Adventures Of Kror

Fun Mazes For Kids Ages 6-8

BRAIN TRAINER

© Copyright 2019 - All rights reserved.

The content contained within this book may not be reproduced, duplicated or transmitted without direct written permission from the author or the publisher.

Under no circumstances will any blame or legal responsibility be held against the publisher, or author, for any damages, reparation, or monetary loss due to the information contained within this book. Either directly or indirectly. You are responsible for your own choices, actions, and results.

Legal Notice:

This book is copyright protected. This book is only for personal use. You cannot amend, distribute, sell, use, quote or paraphrase any part, or the content within this book, without the consent of the author or publisher.

Disclaimer Notice:

Please note the information contained within this document is for educational and entertainment purposes only. All effort has been executed to present accurate, up to date, and reliable, complete information. No warranties of any kind are declared or implied. Readers acknowledge that the author is not engaging in the rendering of legal, financial, medical or professional advice. The content within this book has been derived from various sources. Please consult a licensed professional before attempting any techniques outlined in this book.

By reading this document, the reader agrees that under no circumstances is the author responsible for any losses, direct or indirect, which are incurred as a result of the use of the information contained within this document, including, but not limited to, — errors, omissions, or inaccuracies.

Meet the Grobbles:

Kror   Dran   Crik

Help them establish a home in new lands

Help Kror find a tool
Avoid the waterfall !

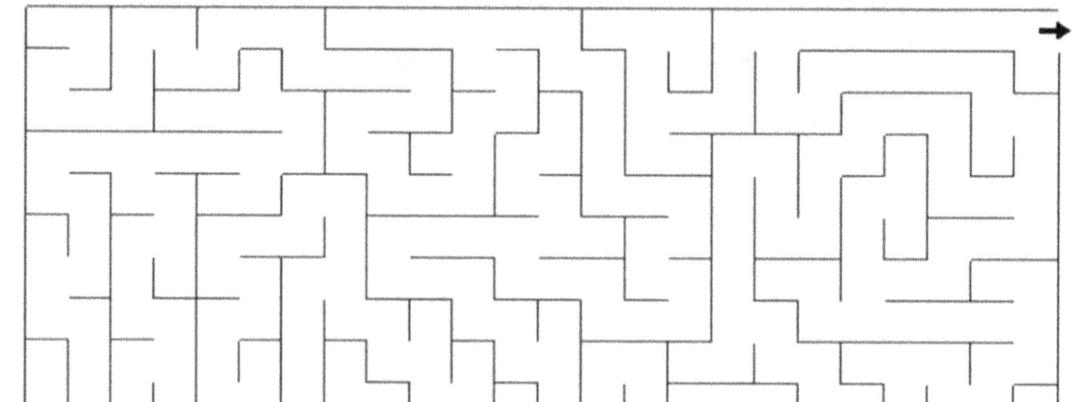

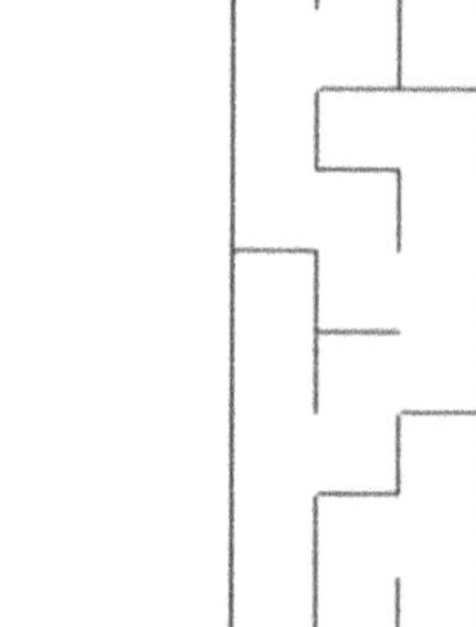

Dran and Crik are hungry. Get to the food

Careful, something else is hungry

Help Kror track down and hunt the bear

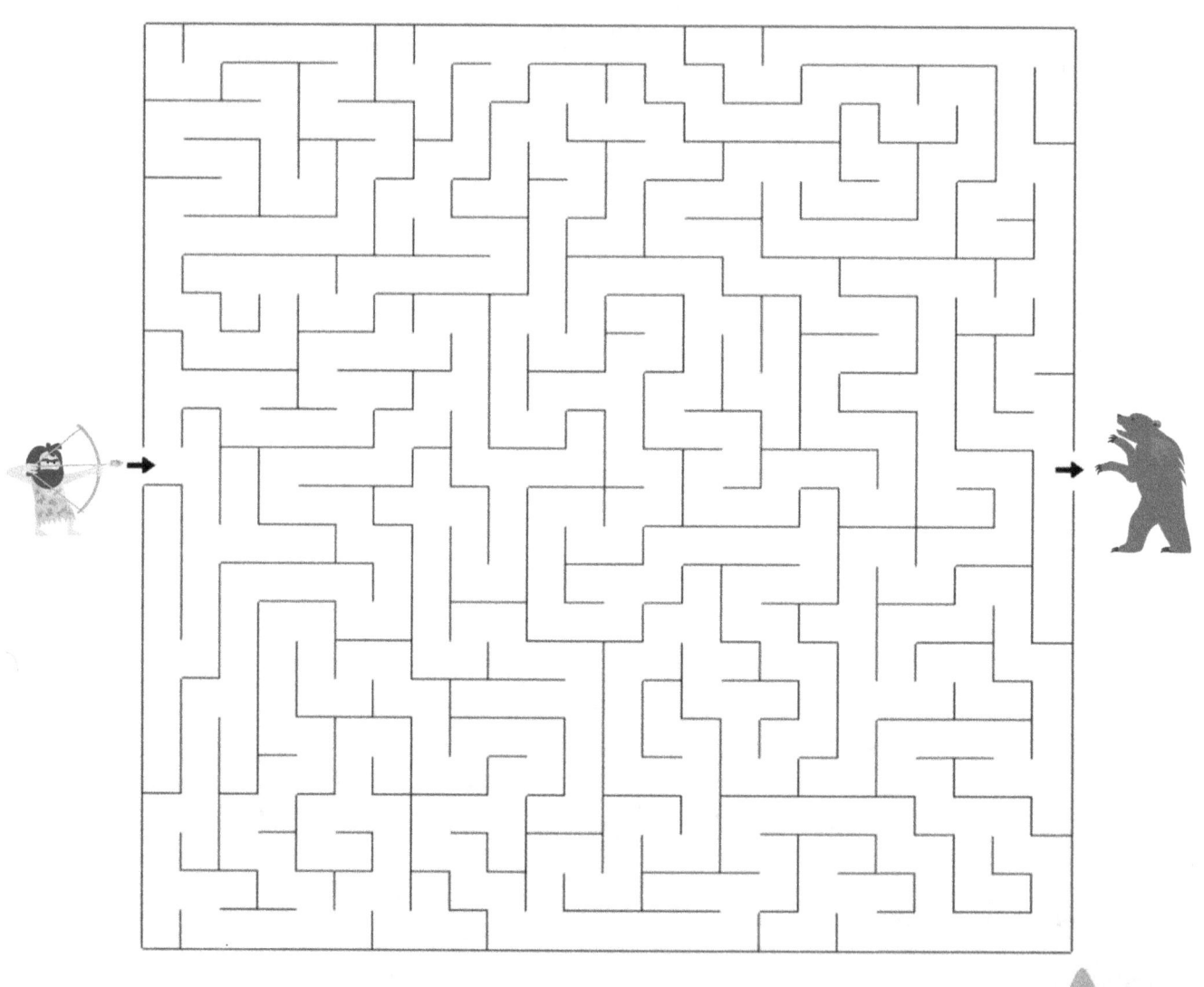

Well done brave Kror, bring the meat to your family

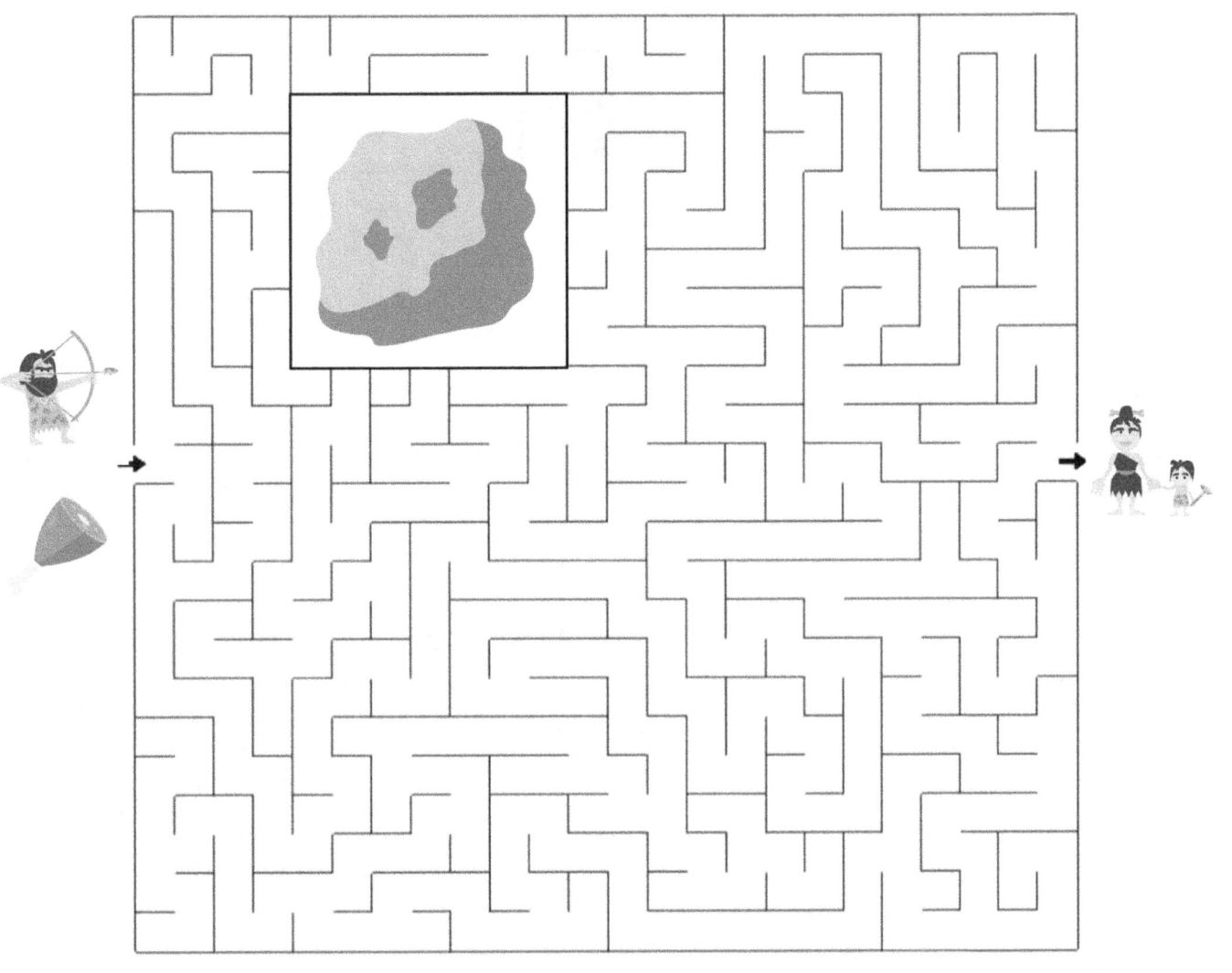

Dran Needs Firewood for fire, Gather the wood and find camp

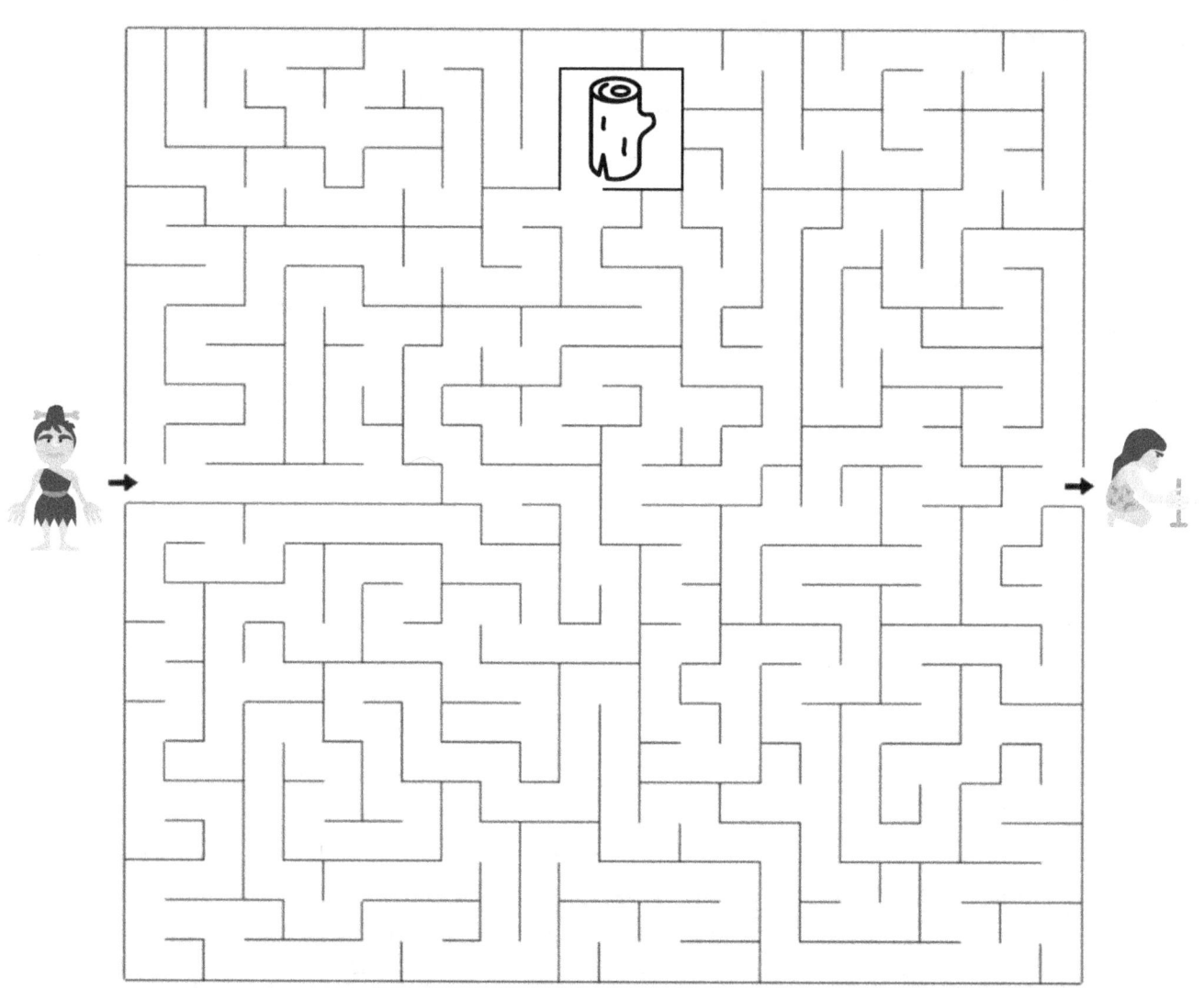

Dran wants to paint an animal, but can't remember what it looks like ! Go find the animal and dscribe it to her

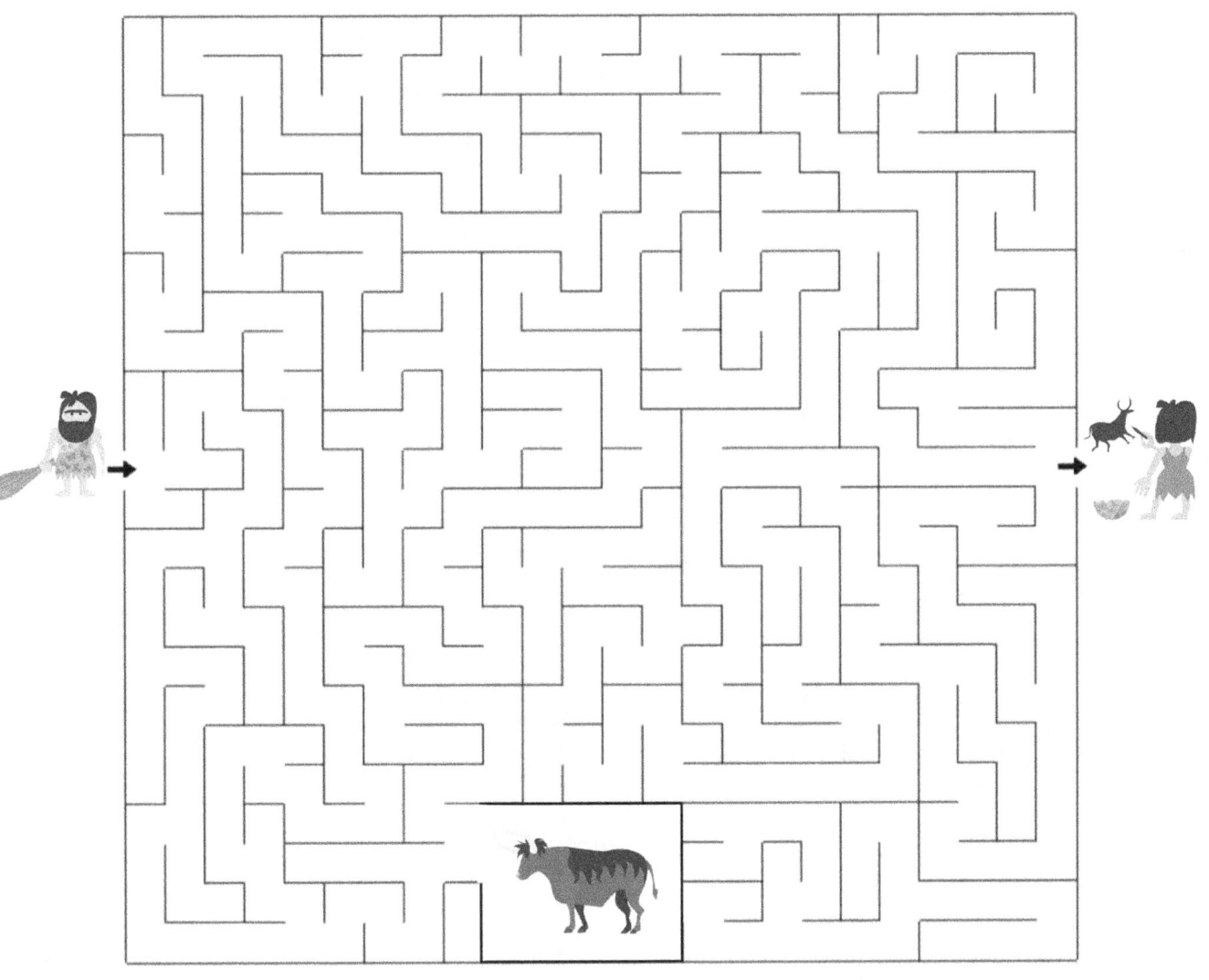

A wild mammoth has appeared !!
Recruit the help of your brother Aruk to defeat it

Time for a day of fishing. Get to the waterfall

Crik is lost, afraid and cold. Help him get home so he can be warm once again.

Dran lost her necklace.. She thinks she dropped it this morning. Go find it for her

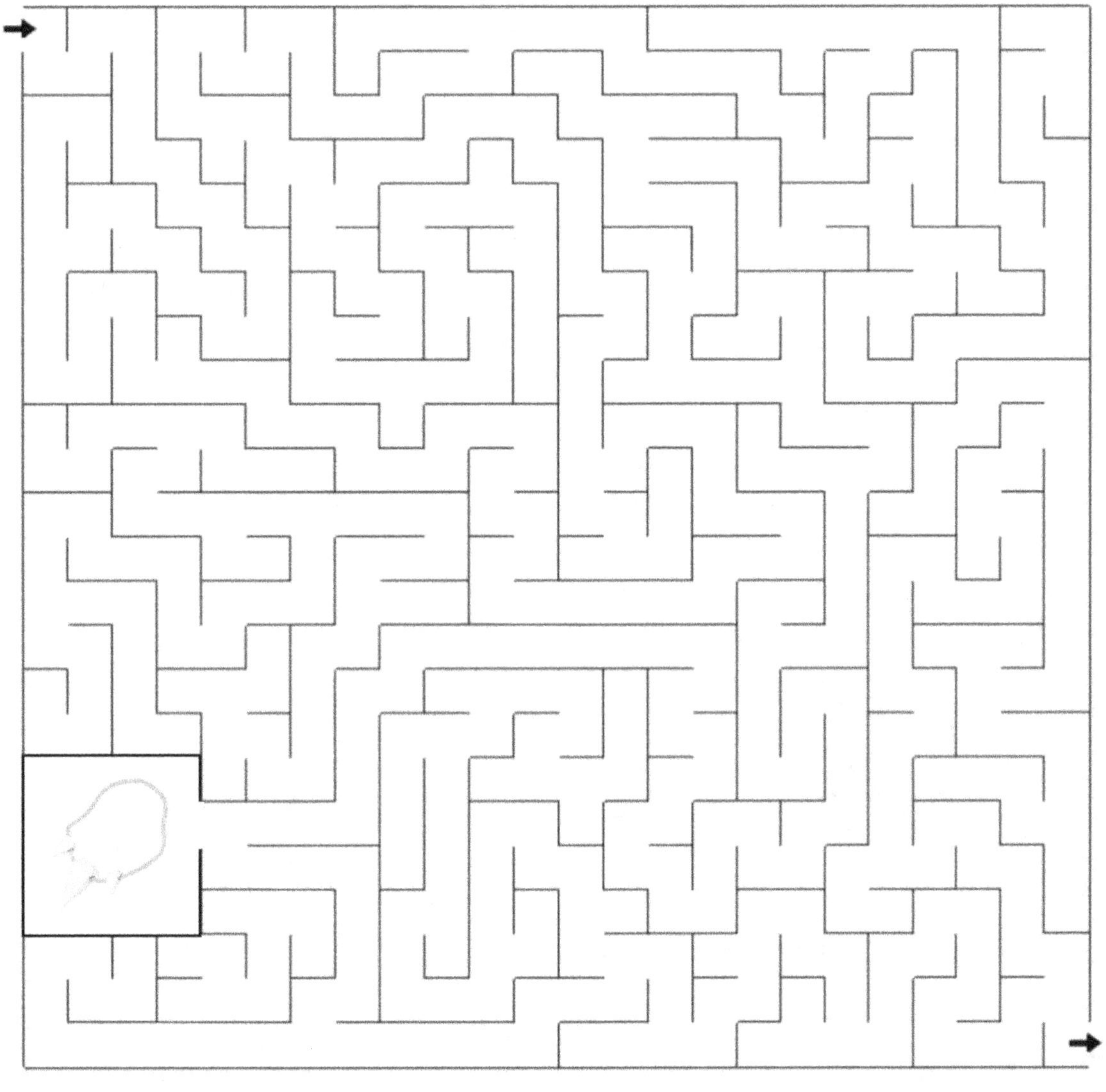

Gather the material to make Crik his first spear !

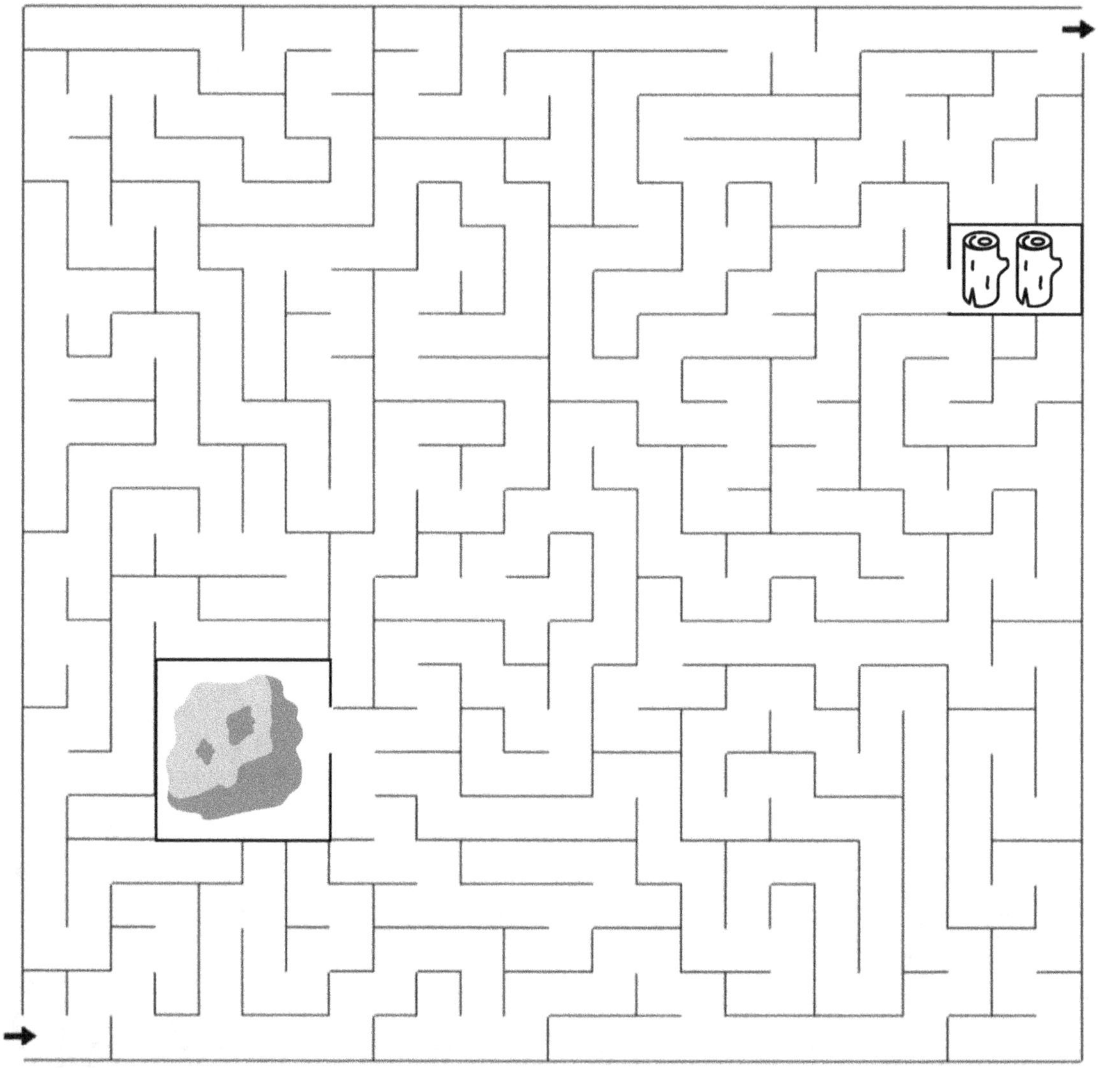

Take Crik on his first hunting trip

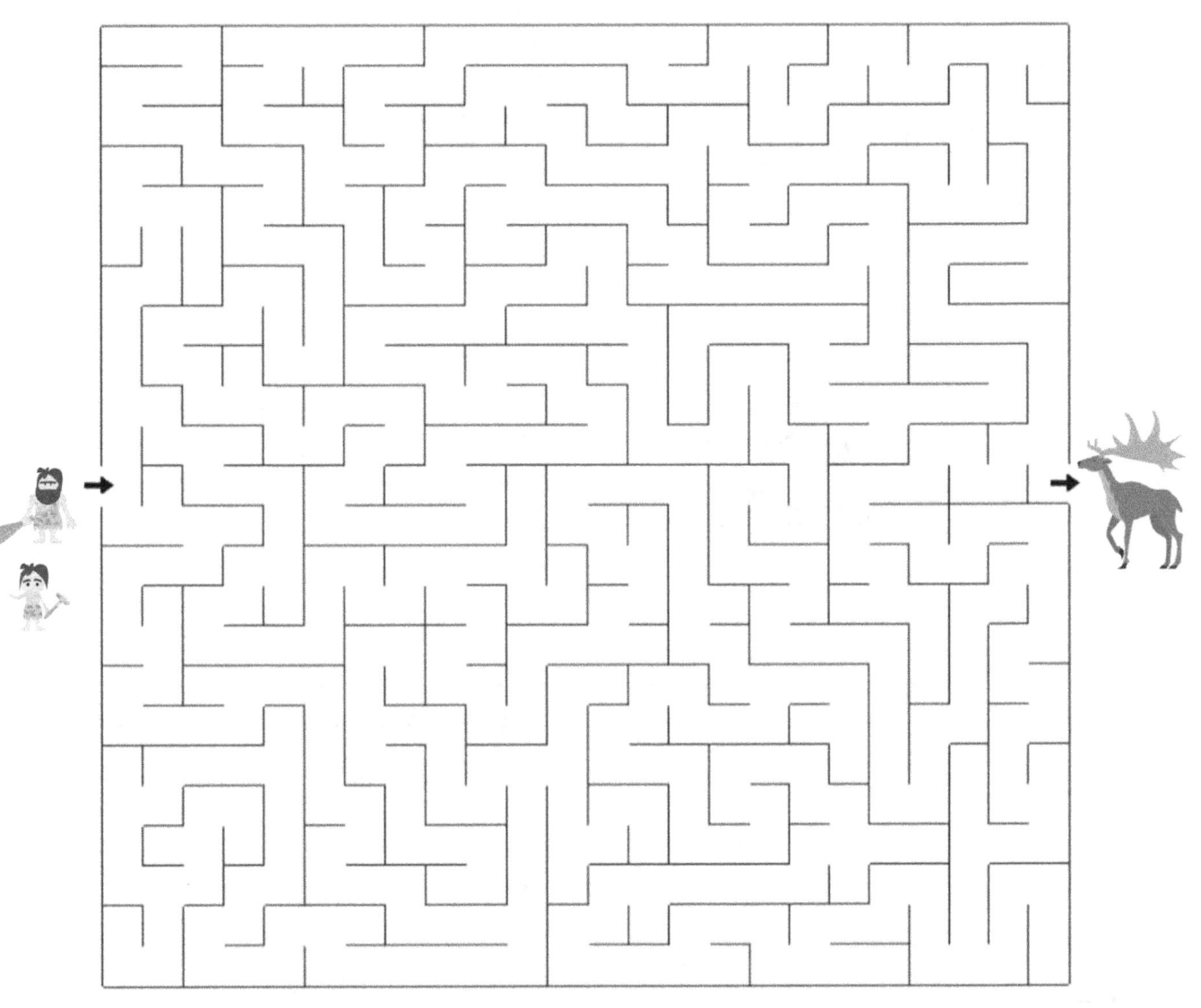

Dran must prepare the fire for Kror and Crik. Help her get more wood.

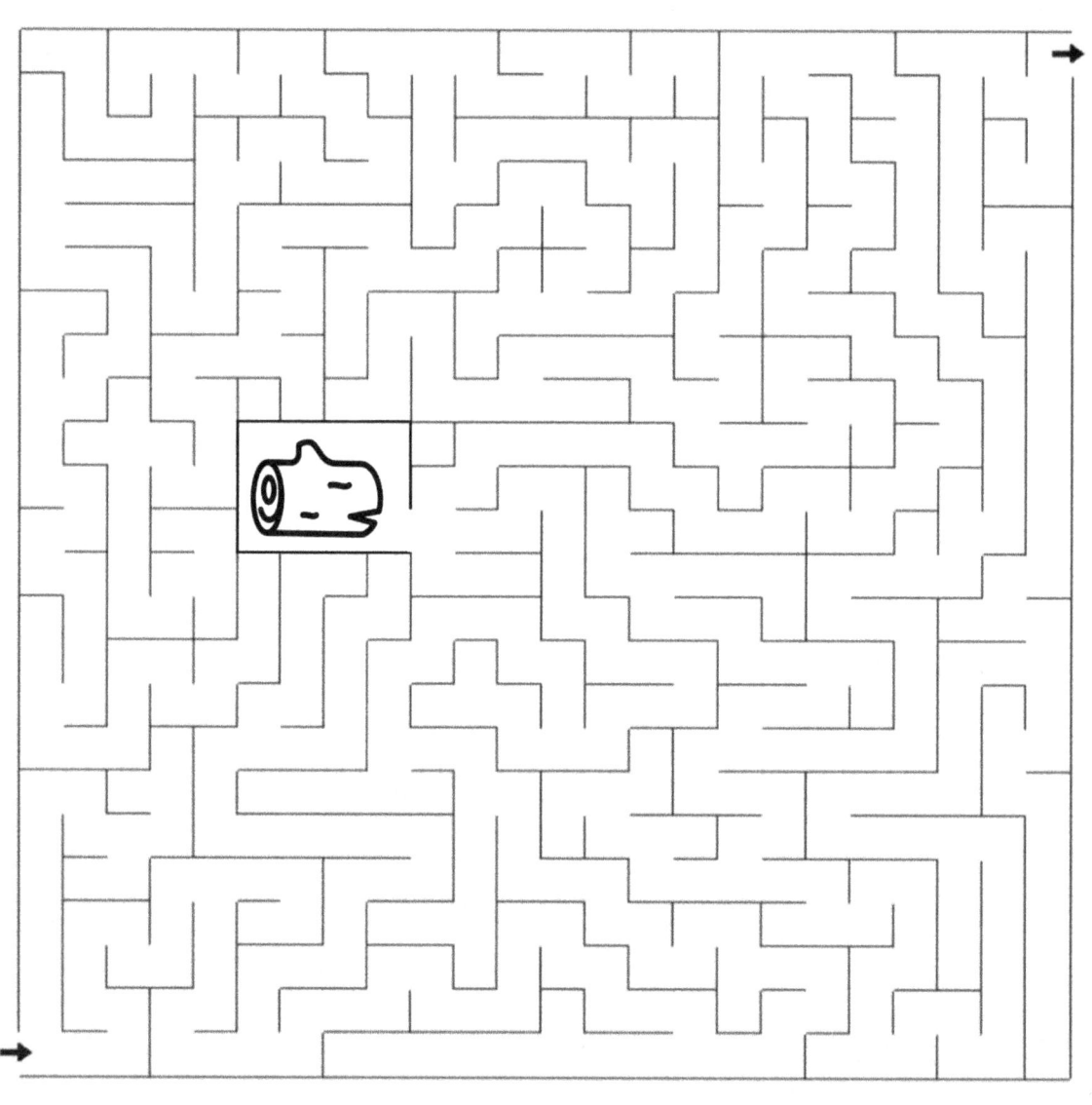

Crik now needs to learn to cook, help him find the fire Dran has prepared

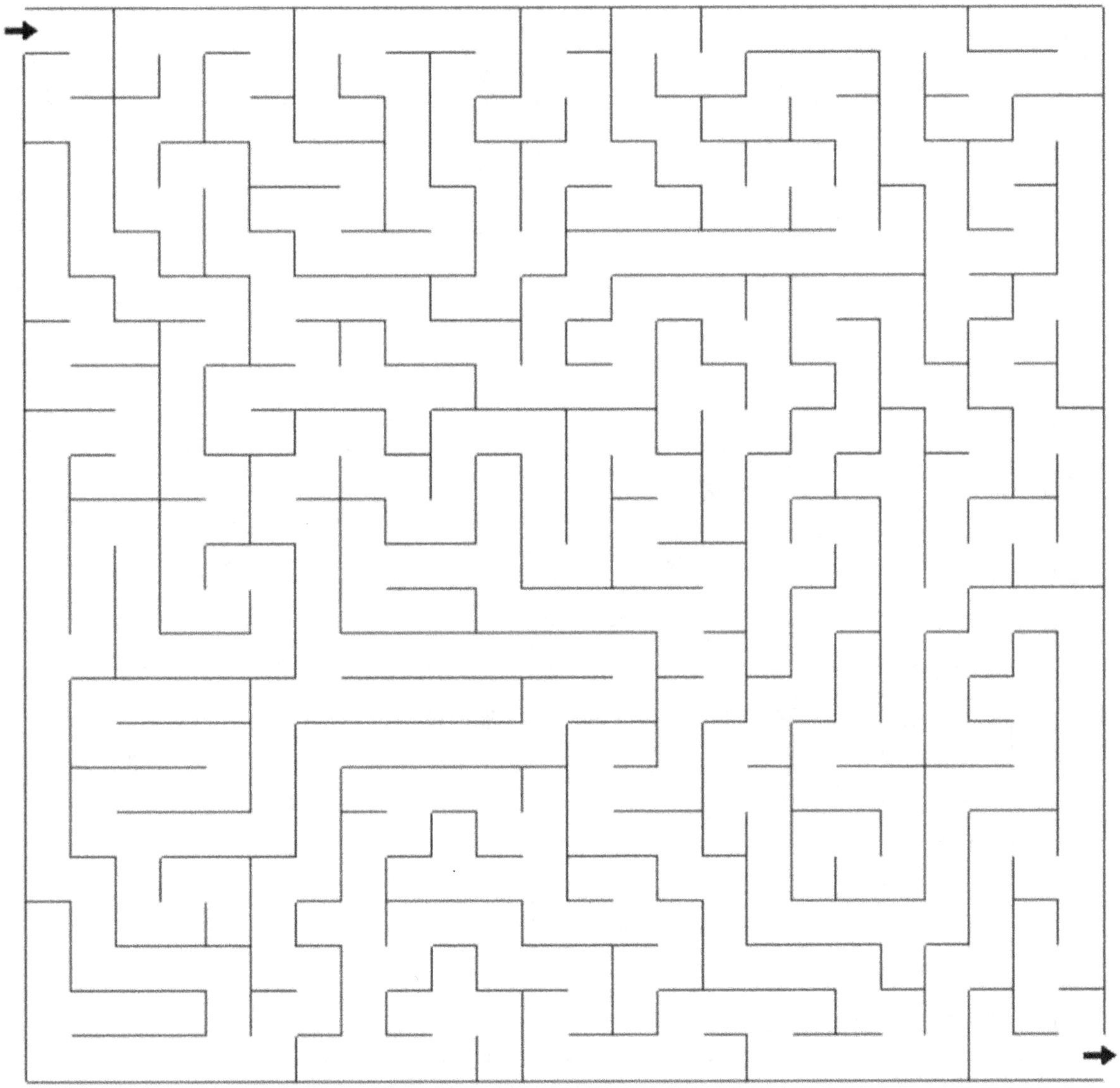

Kror built a tree house for Crik deep in the forest. Help Crik find it!

Kror's brother Aruk is in danger, rush to his rescue

Food sources are getting low. Dran heard of a new grain that grows well. Find it and plant it.

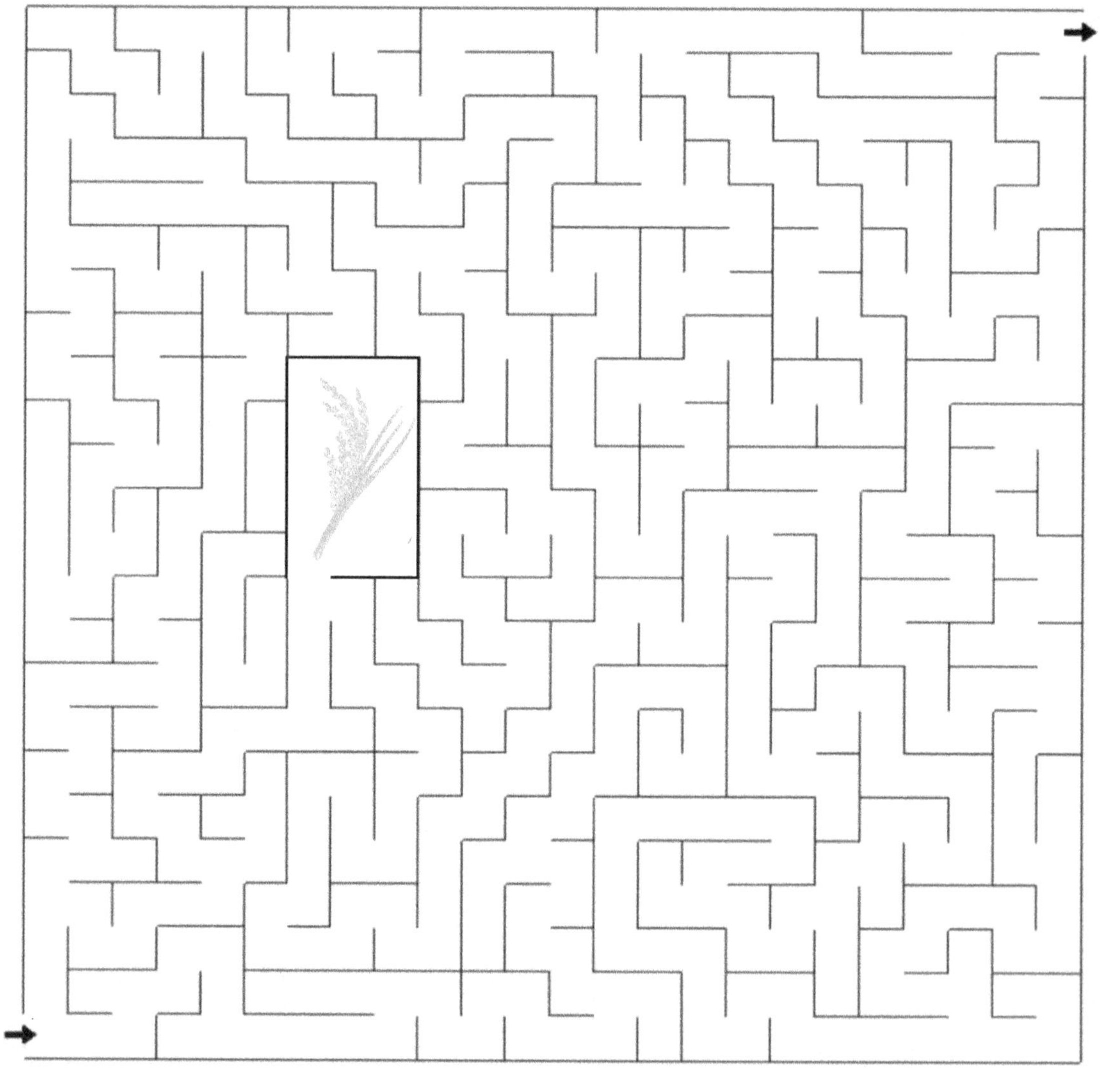

Kror tamed an animal for use in growing crops. Help Kror take the animal back to camp

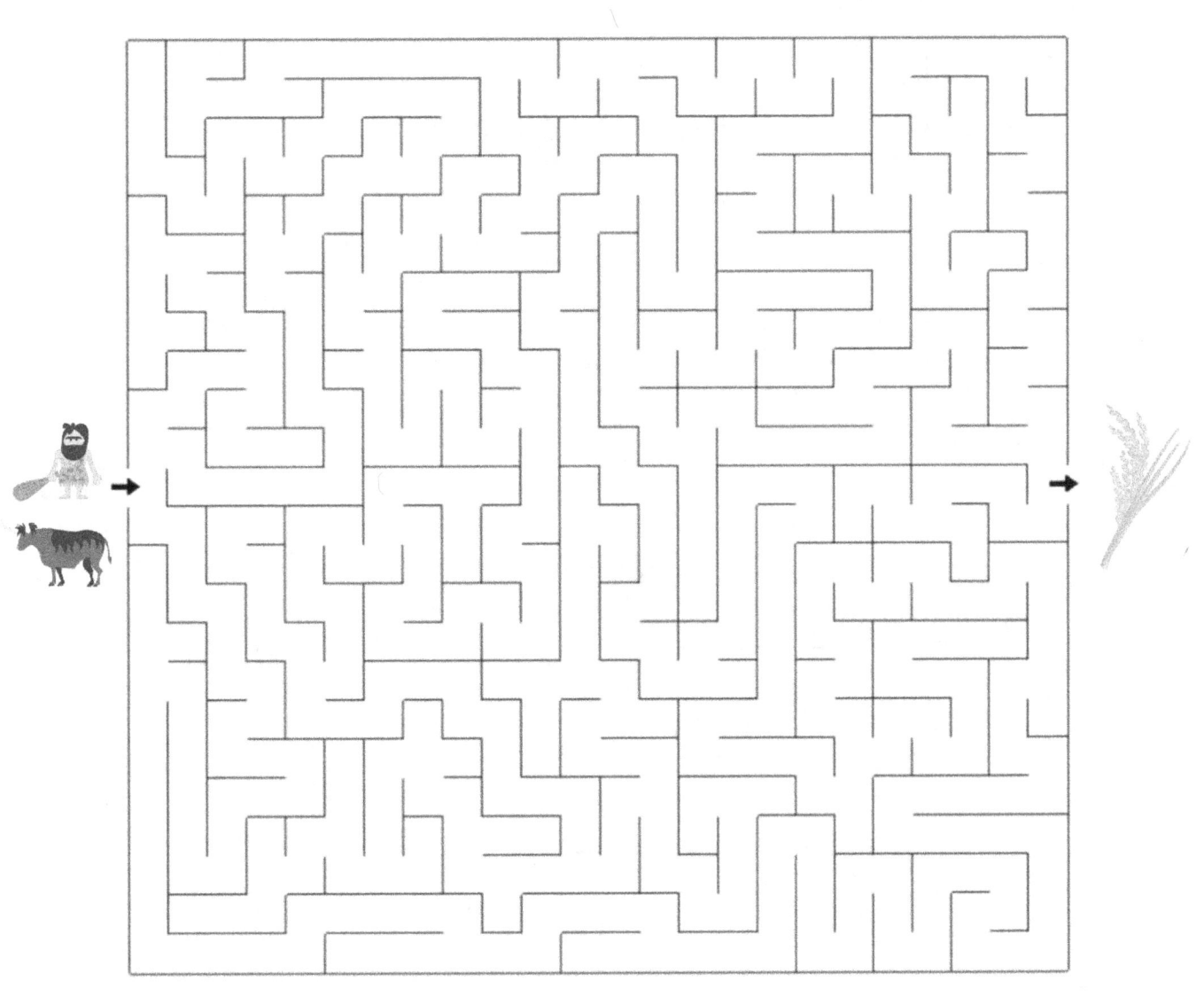

Terrible rains are coming and their animal has run off! Find the animal and get the Grobbles to safety in a nearby cave

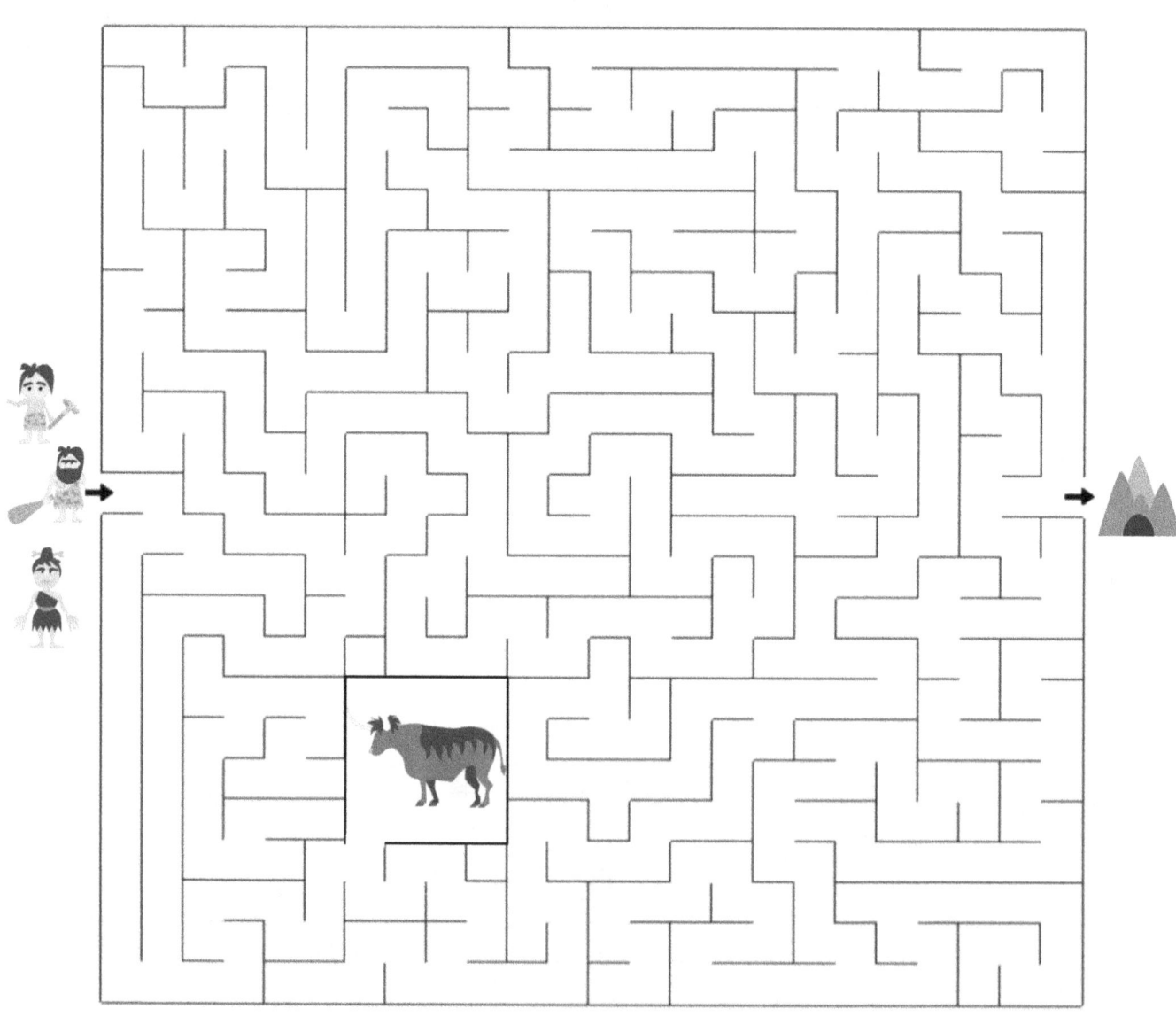

The land is filling with water too quickly ! Cross the river and find new land

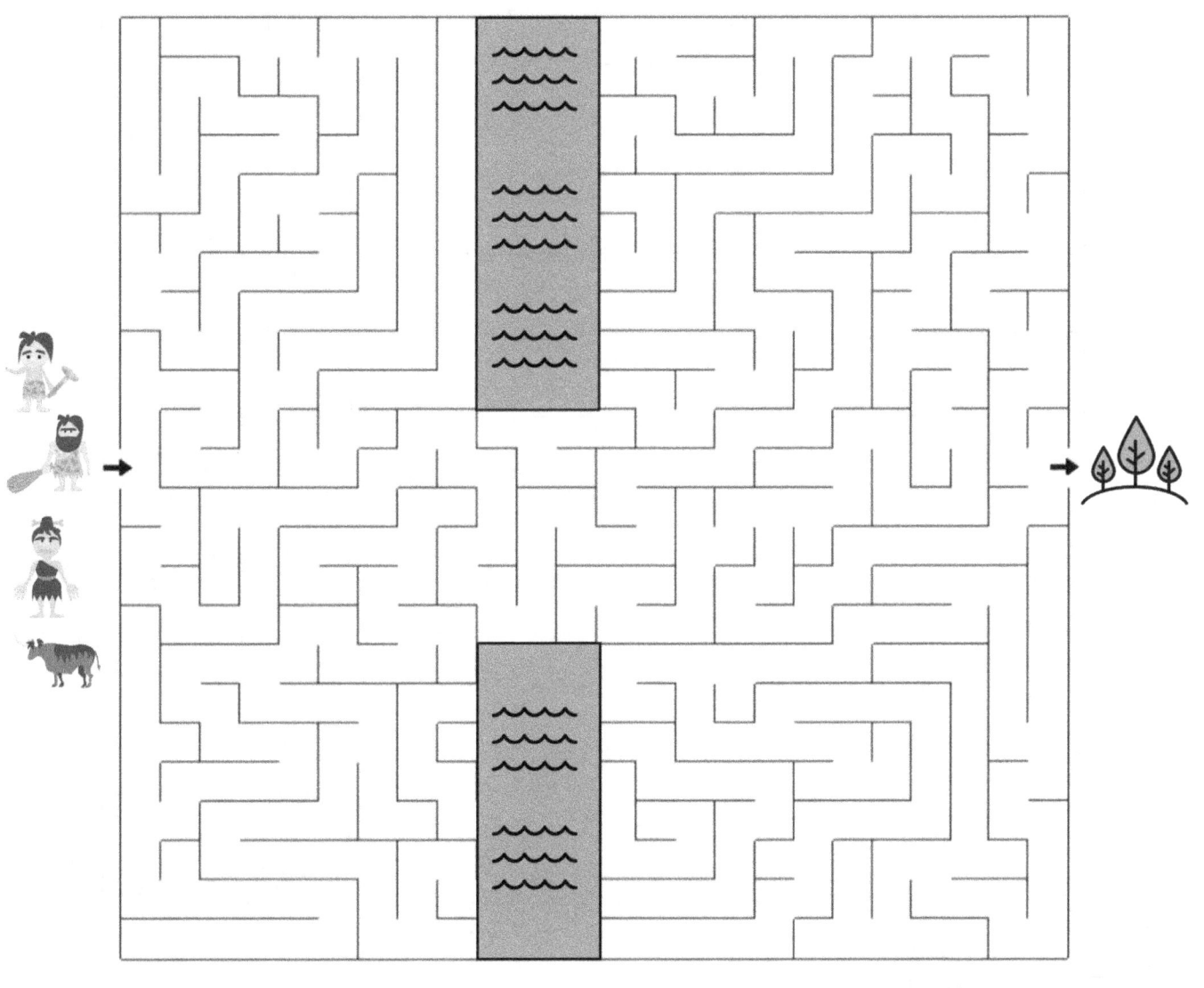

The wetlands are difficult to navigate. Avoid the crocodiles and find the big tree for shelter

Dran spotted a tree with new fruit on the way to the big tree ! Go back and fetch some fruit

Careful of the larger creatures here

Crik has fallen into a pond in the new wetlands, help him swim to safety

Aruk tried to follow the Grobbles family to the new big tree but got lost along the way. Help him find his way

Crik is scared of the new larger creatures. Go scare them off

With all of their crops washed away, Crik wants to release their tamed animal. Find a safe place to do so

Kror wants to surprise Dran with a rare flower. Go deeper in the forest and find it

Kror needs to find some vine to help put a new shelter together. Navigate through the palm trees to find some

Legend says a 'Great Axe' is hidden inside a cave. Help Kror find the cave

Careful of the big cats

You found the cave. The Great Axe is near but avoid the biting bats !

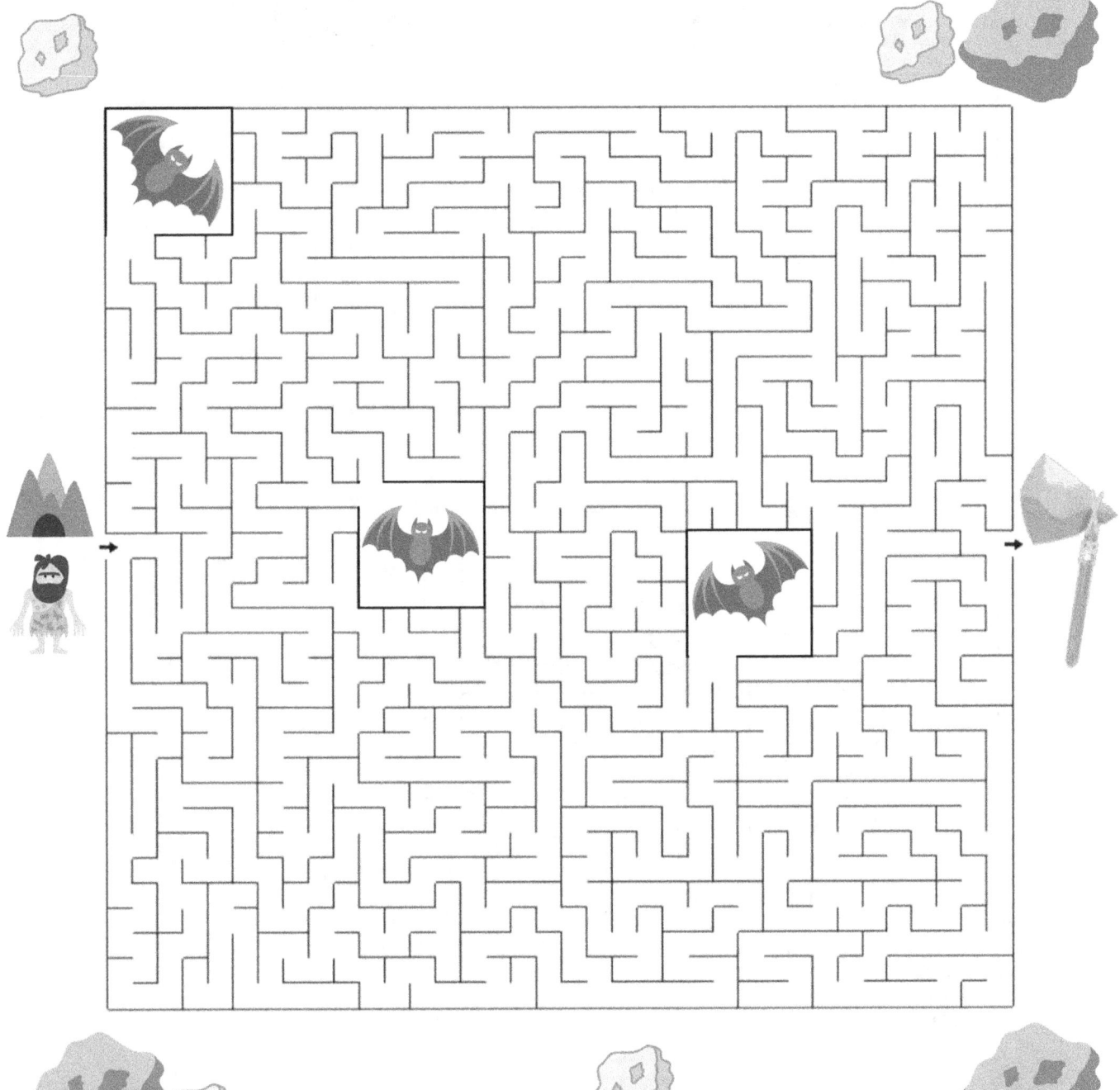

Help Kror find a tool
Avoid the waterfall !

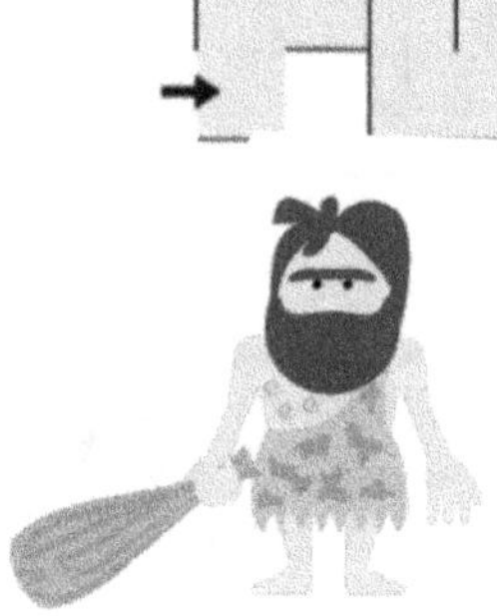

Dran and Crik are hungry. Get to the food

Careful, something else is hungry

Help Kror track down and hunt the bear

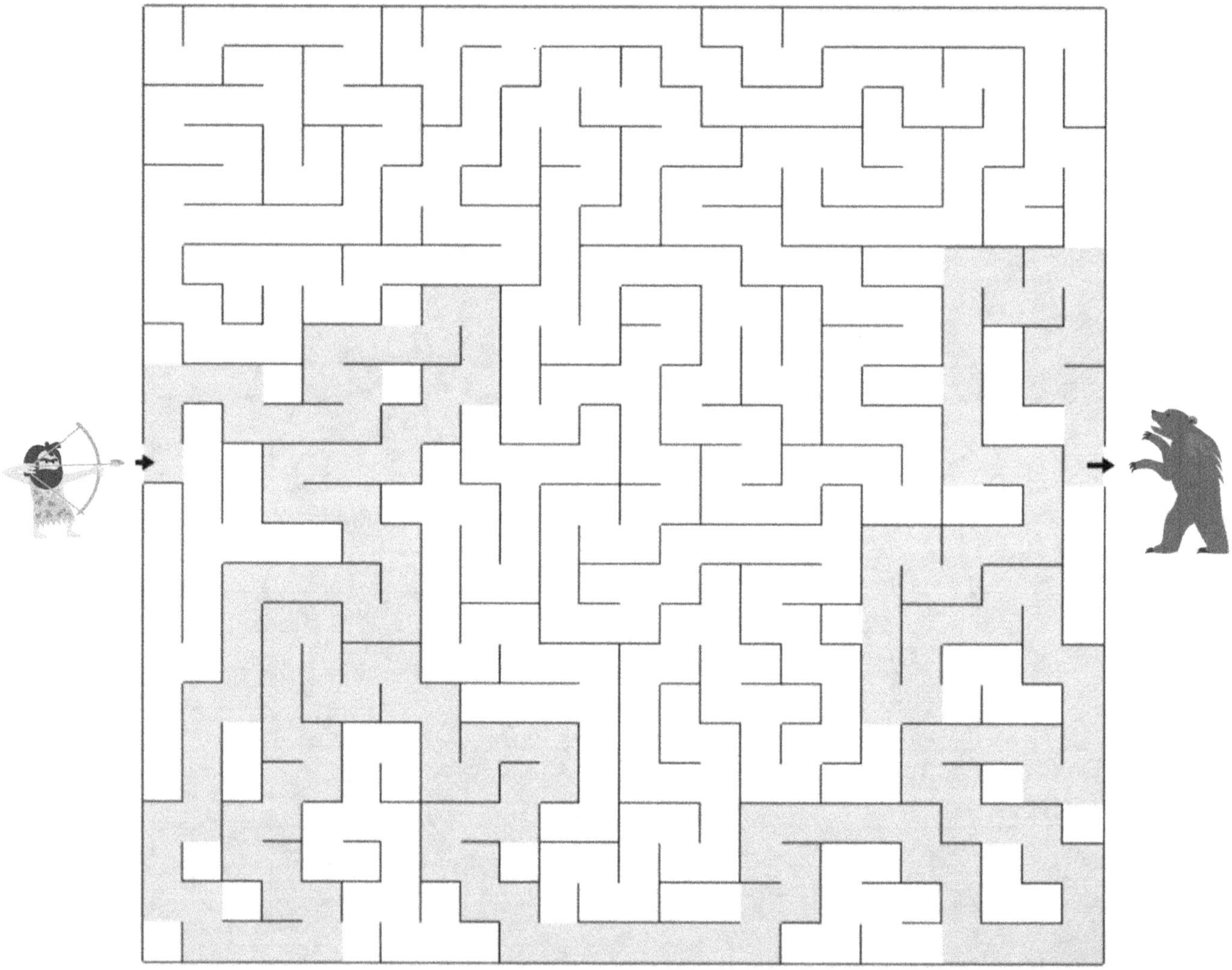

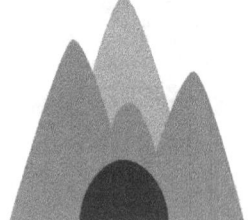

Well done brave Kror, bring the meat to your family

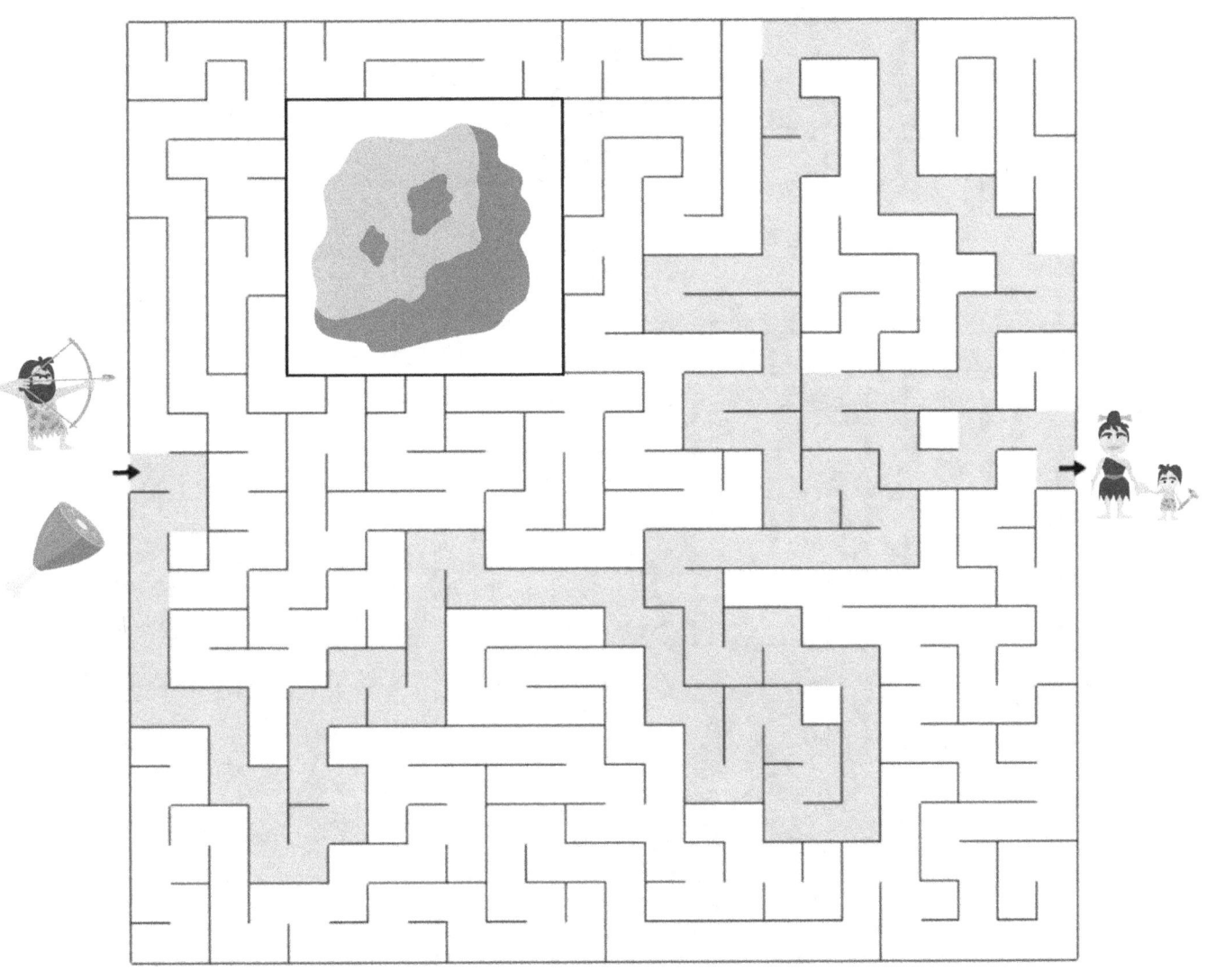

Dran Needs Firewood for fire, Gather the wood and find camp

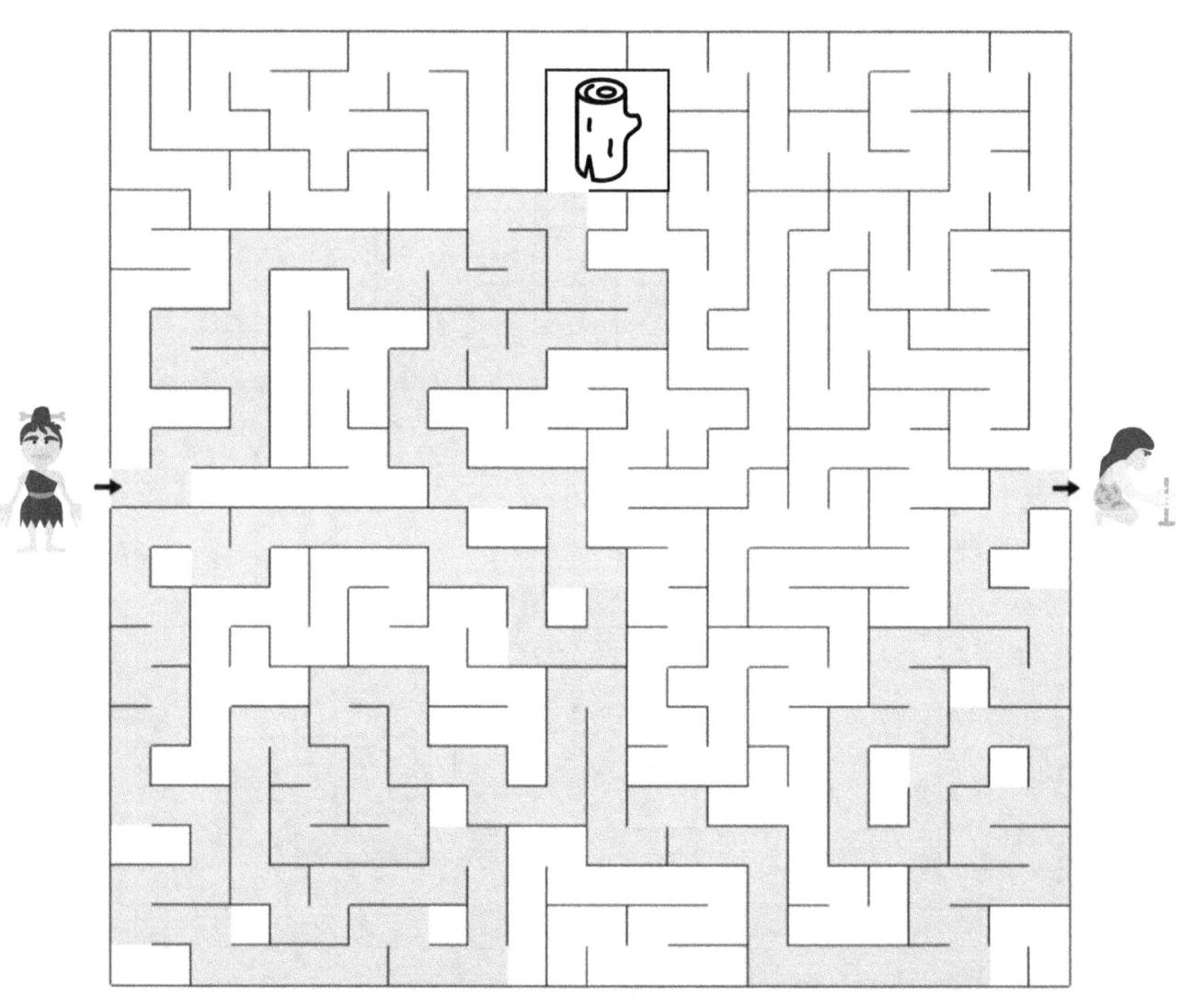

Dran wants to paint an animal, but can't remember what it looks like ! Go find the animal and dscribe it to her

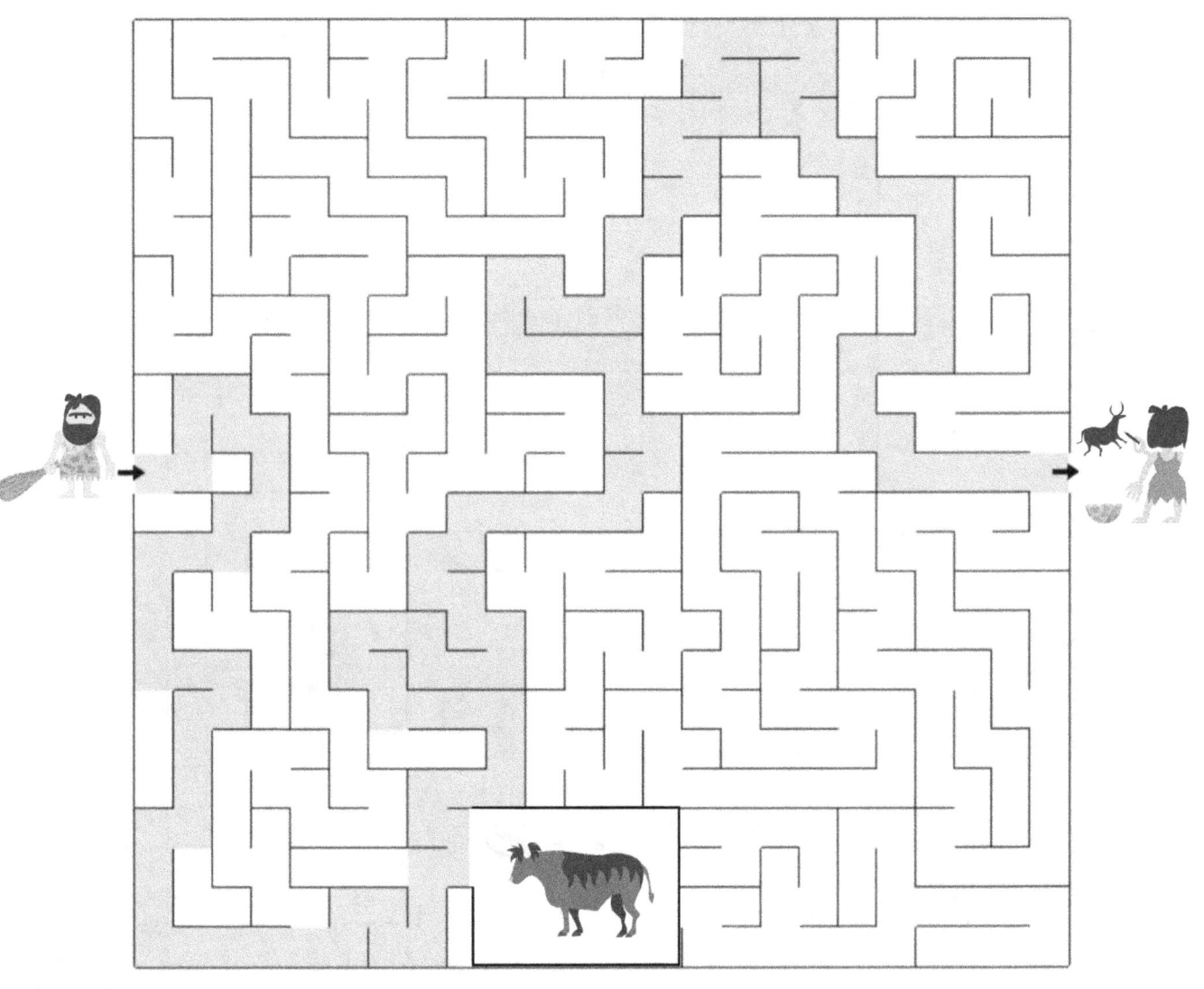

A wild mammoth has appeared !!
Recruit the help of your brother Aruk to defeat it

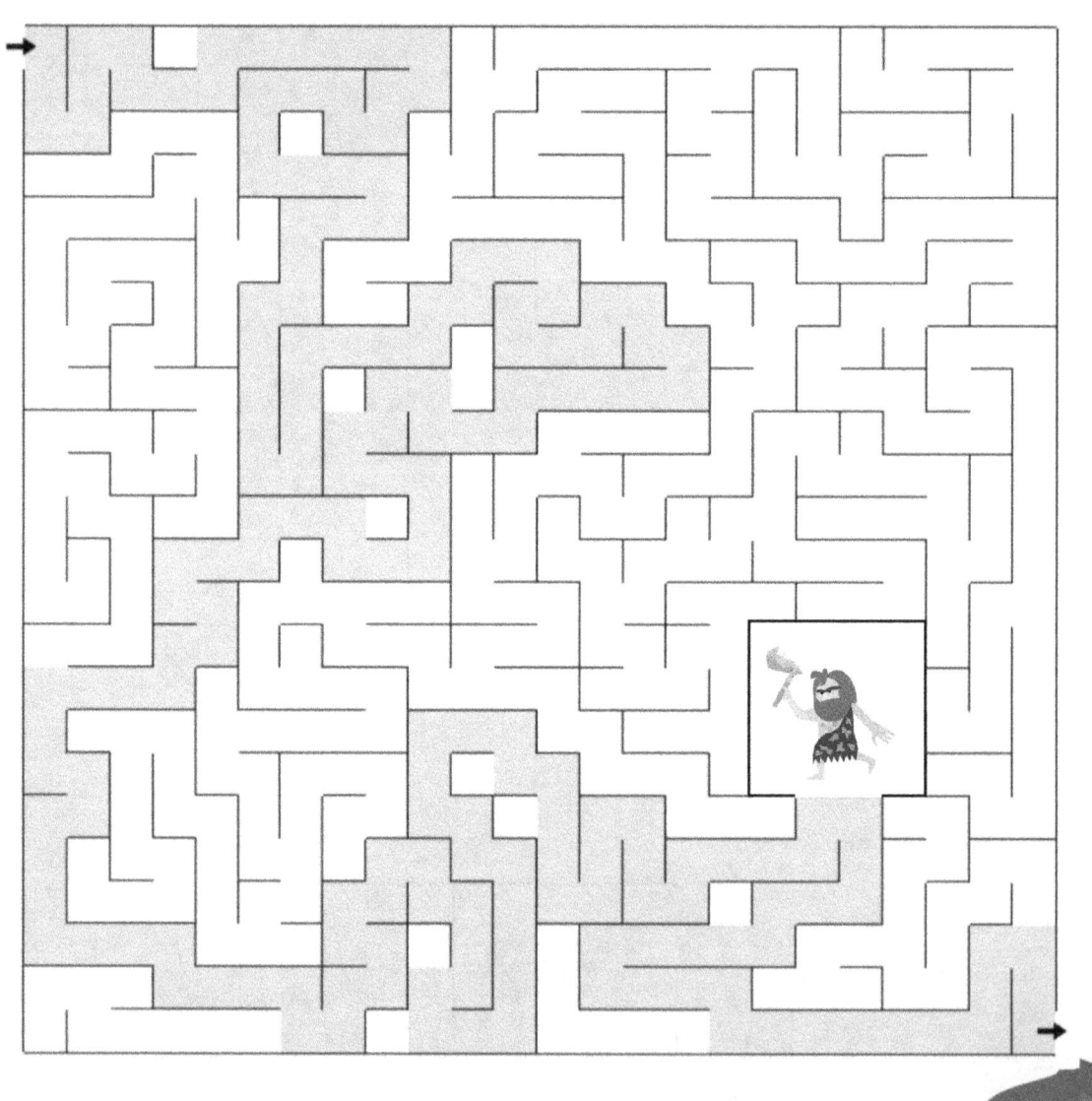

Time for a day of fishing. Get to the waterfall

Crik is lost, afraid and cold. Help him get home so he can be warm once again.

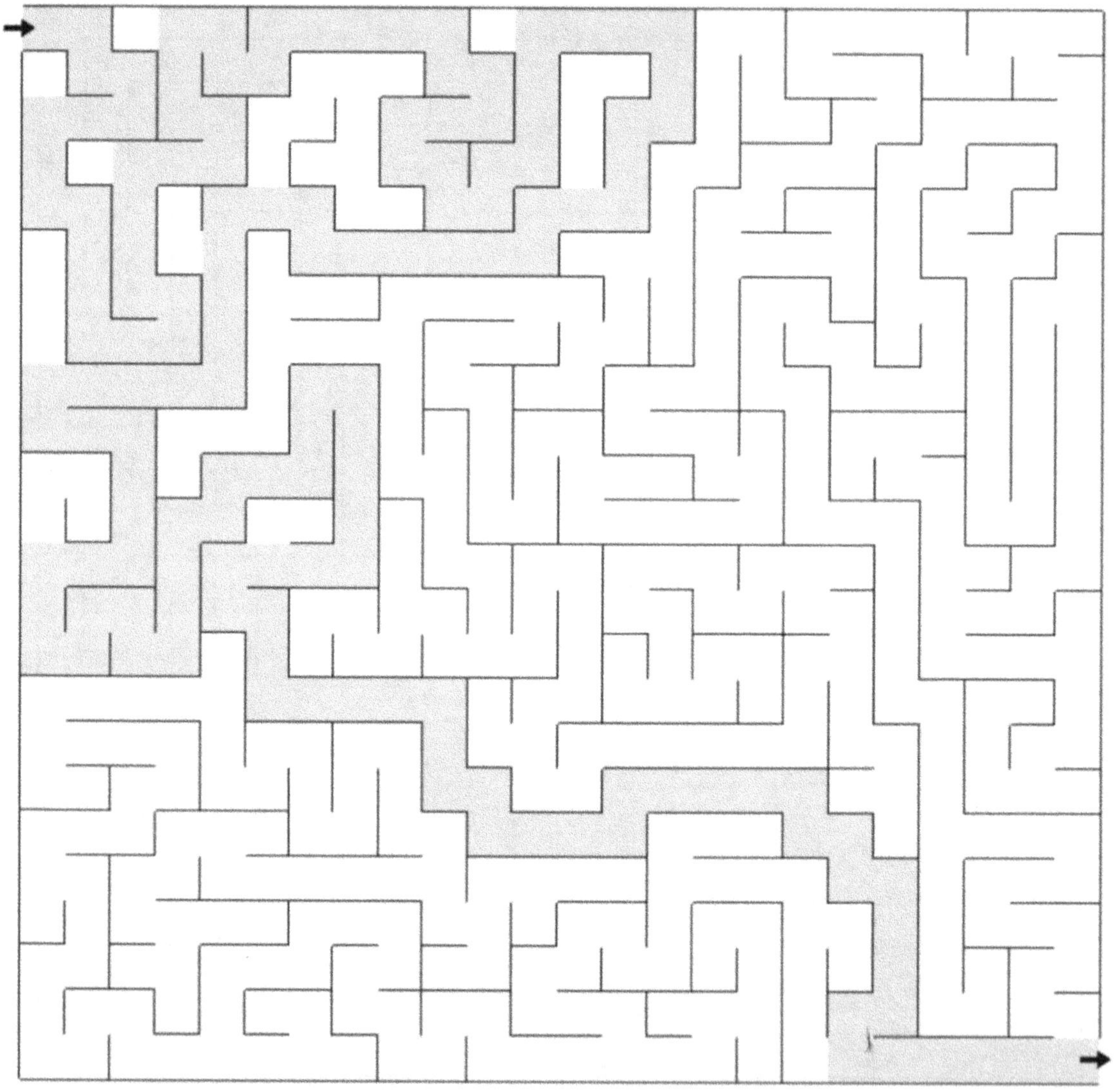

Dran lost her necklace.. She thinks she dropped it this morning. Go find it for her

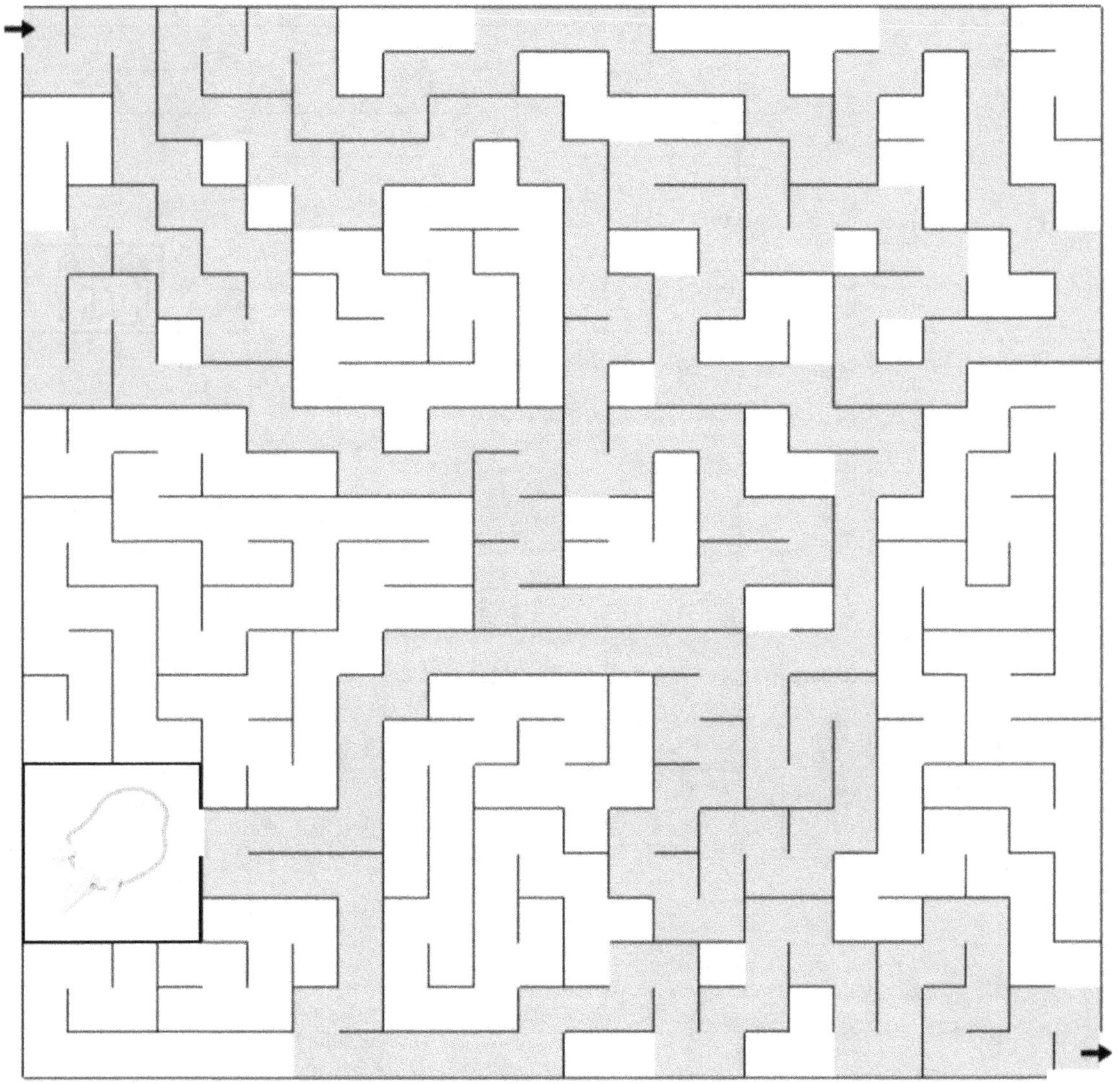

Gather the material to make Crik his first spear !

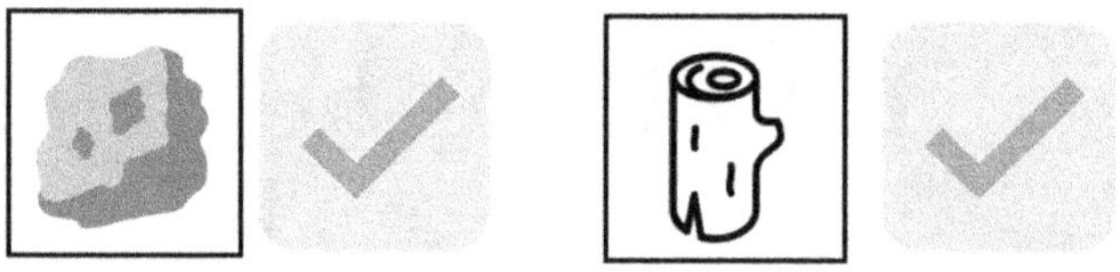

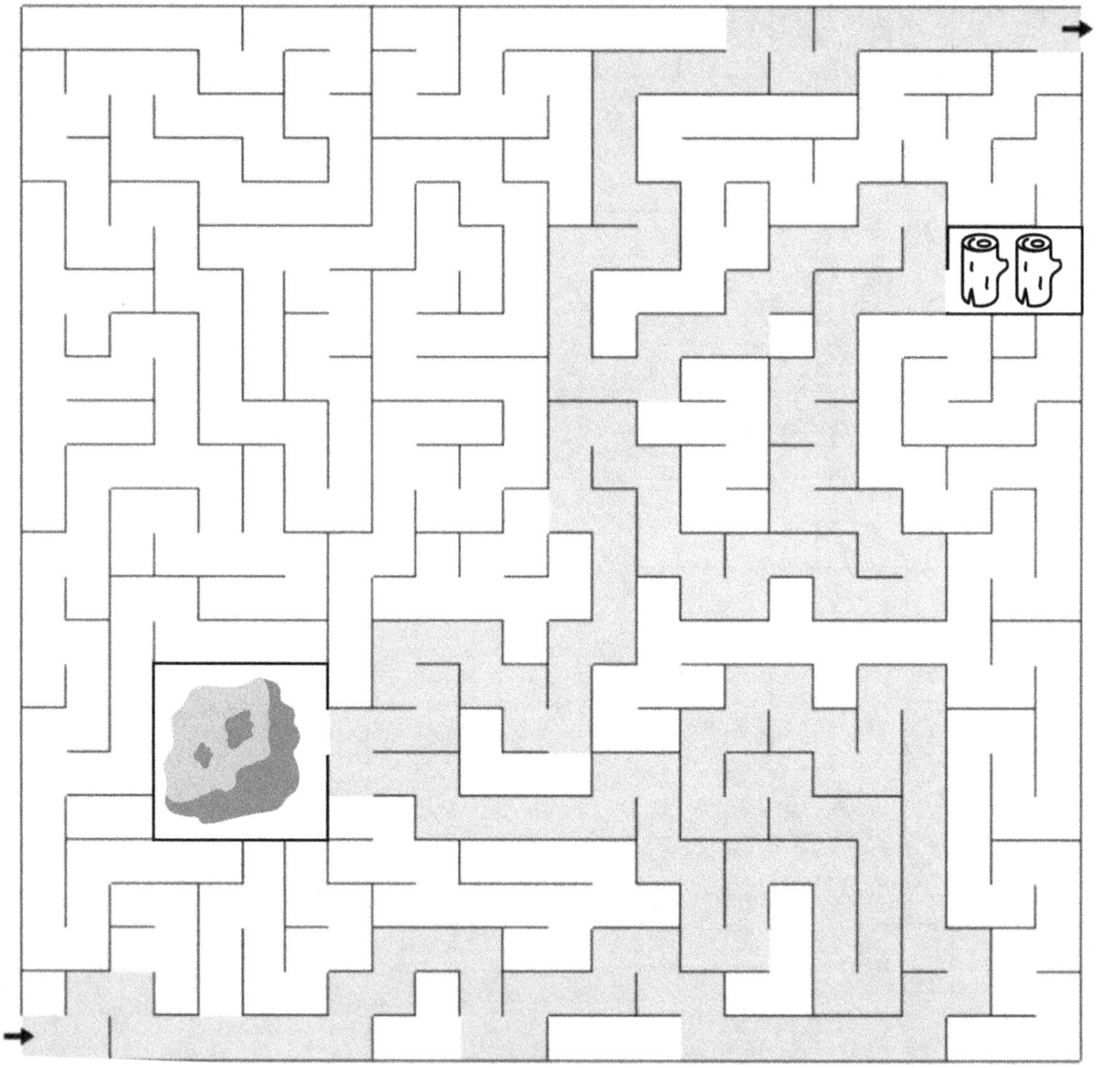

Take Crik on his first hunting trip

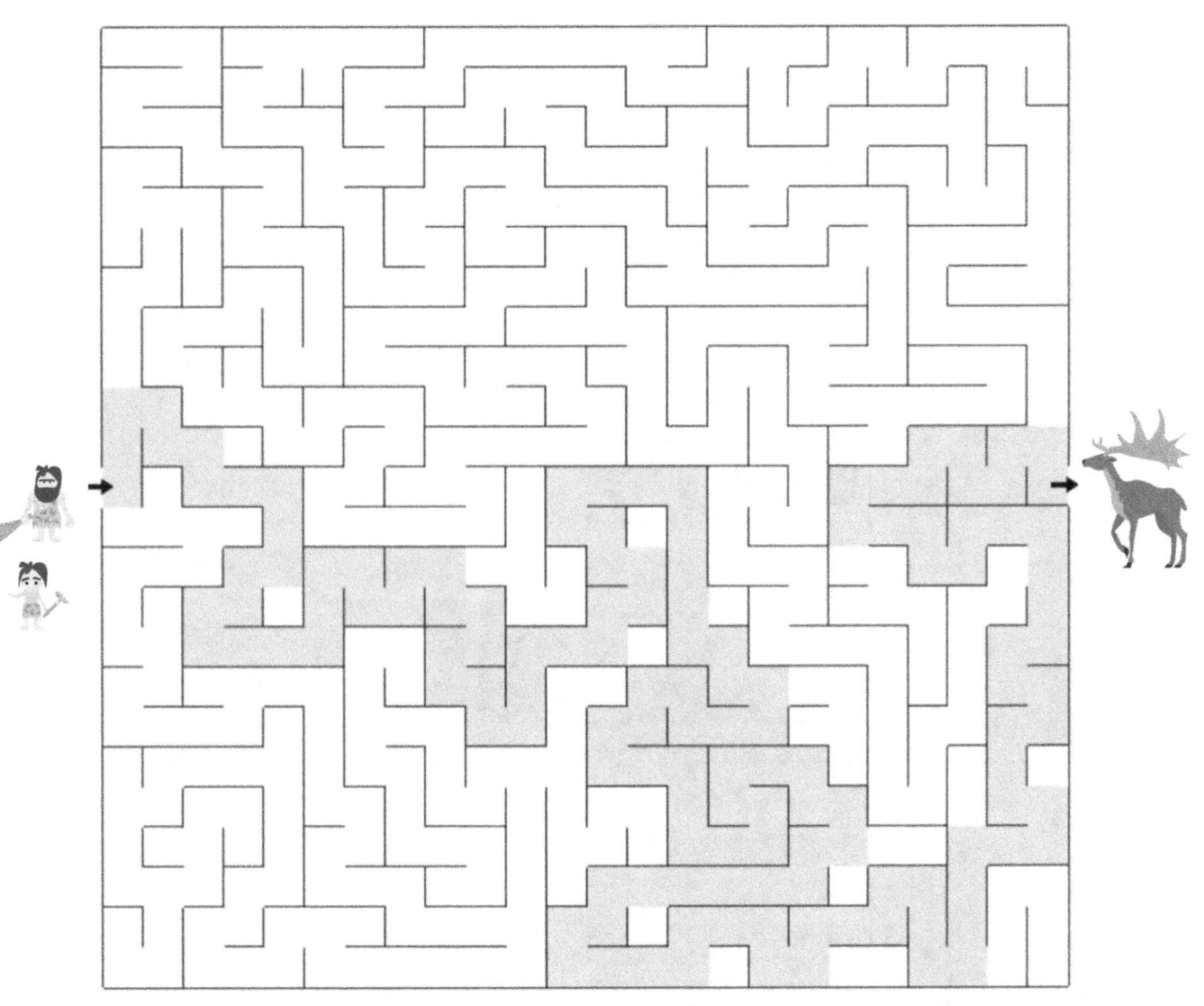

Dran must prepare the fire for Kror and Crik. Help her get more wood.

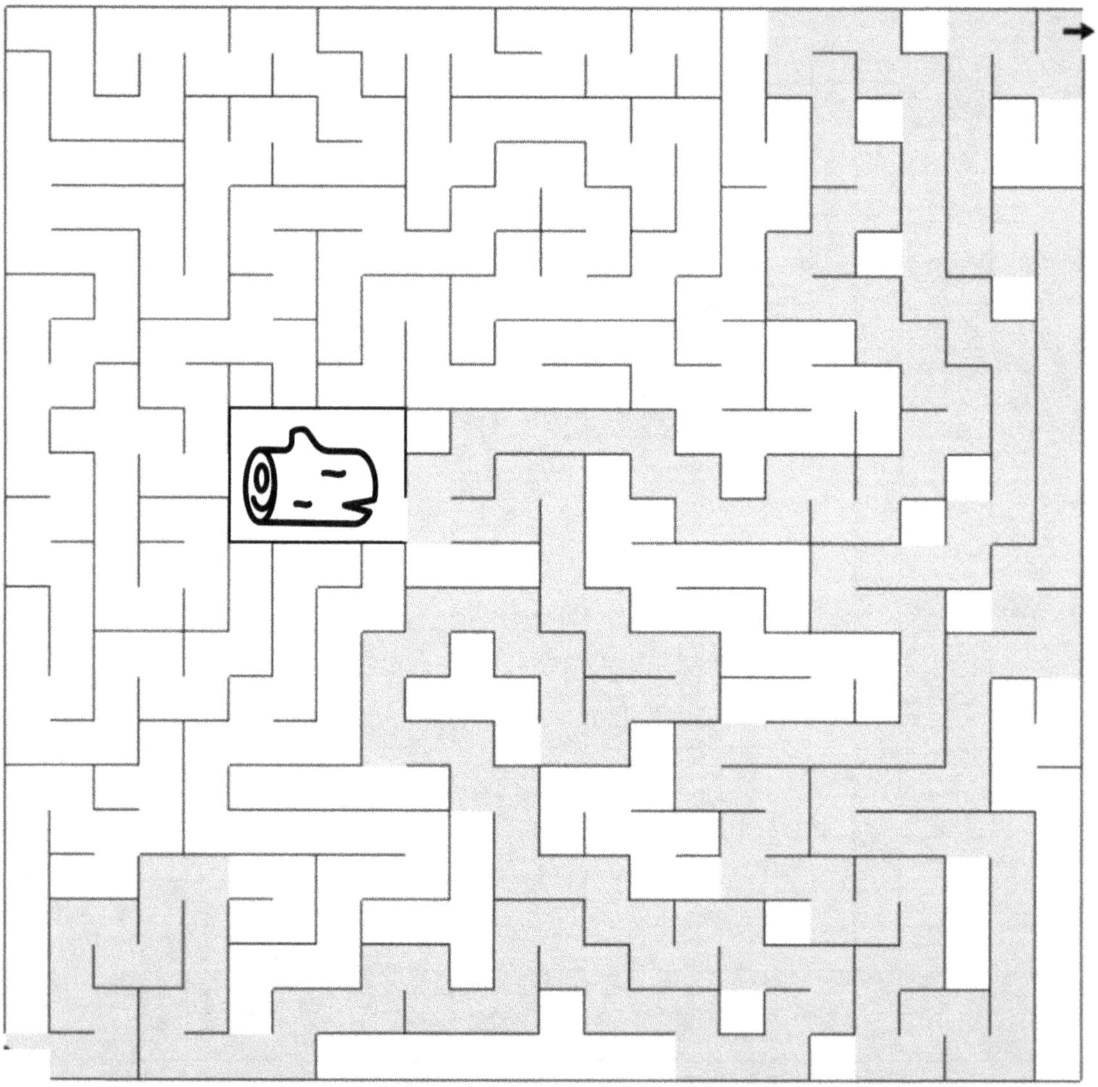

Crik now needs to learn to cook, help him find the fire Dran has prepared

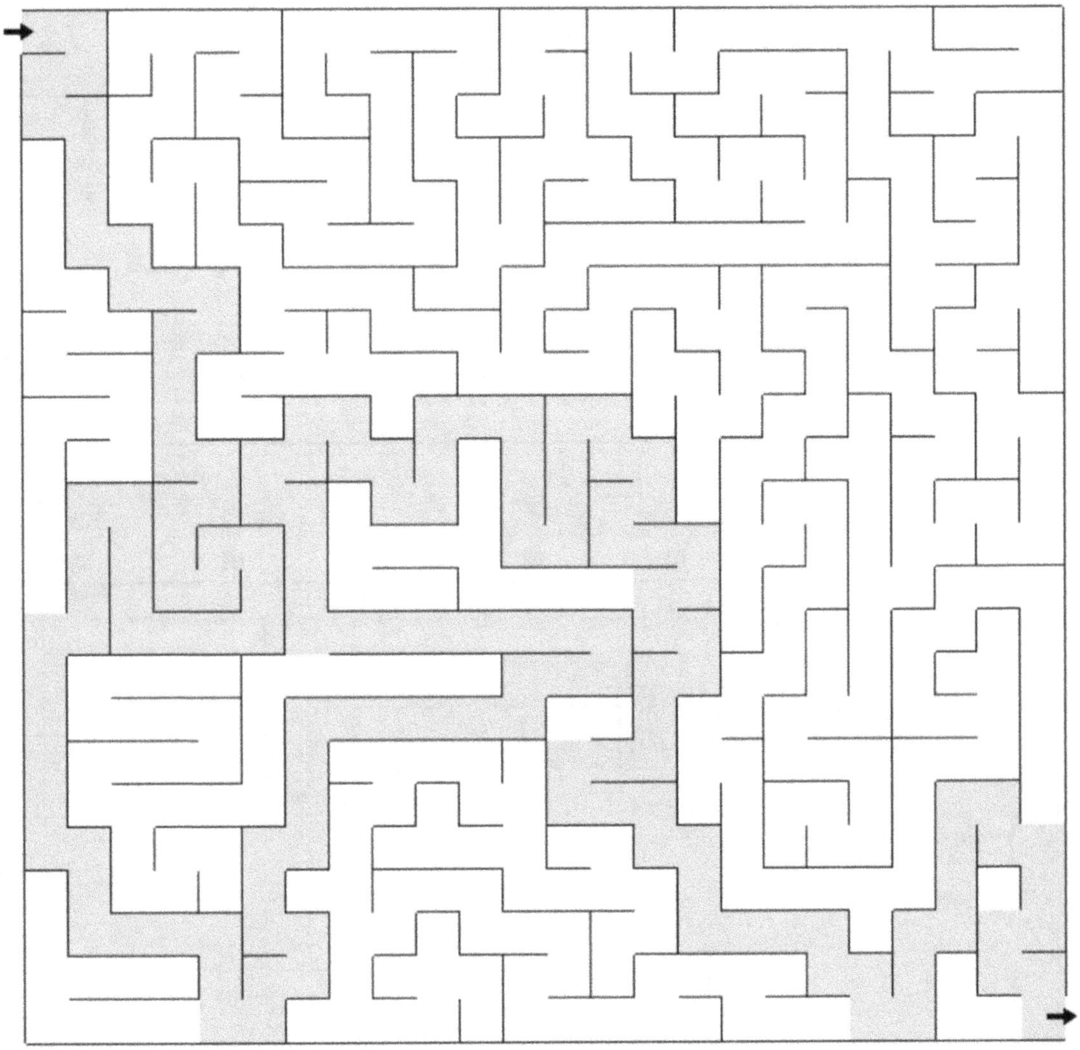

Kror built a tree house for Crik deep in the forest. Help Crik find it!

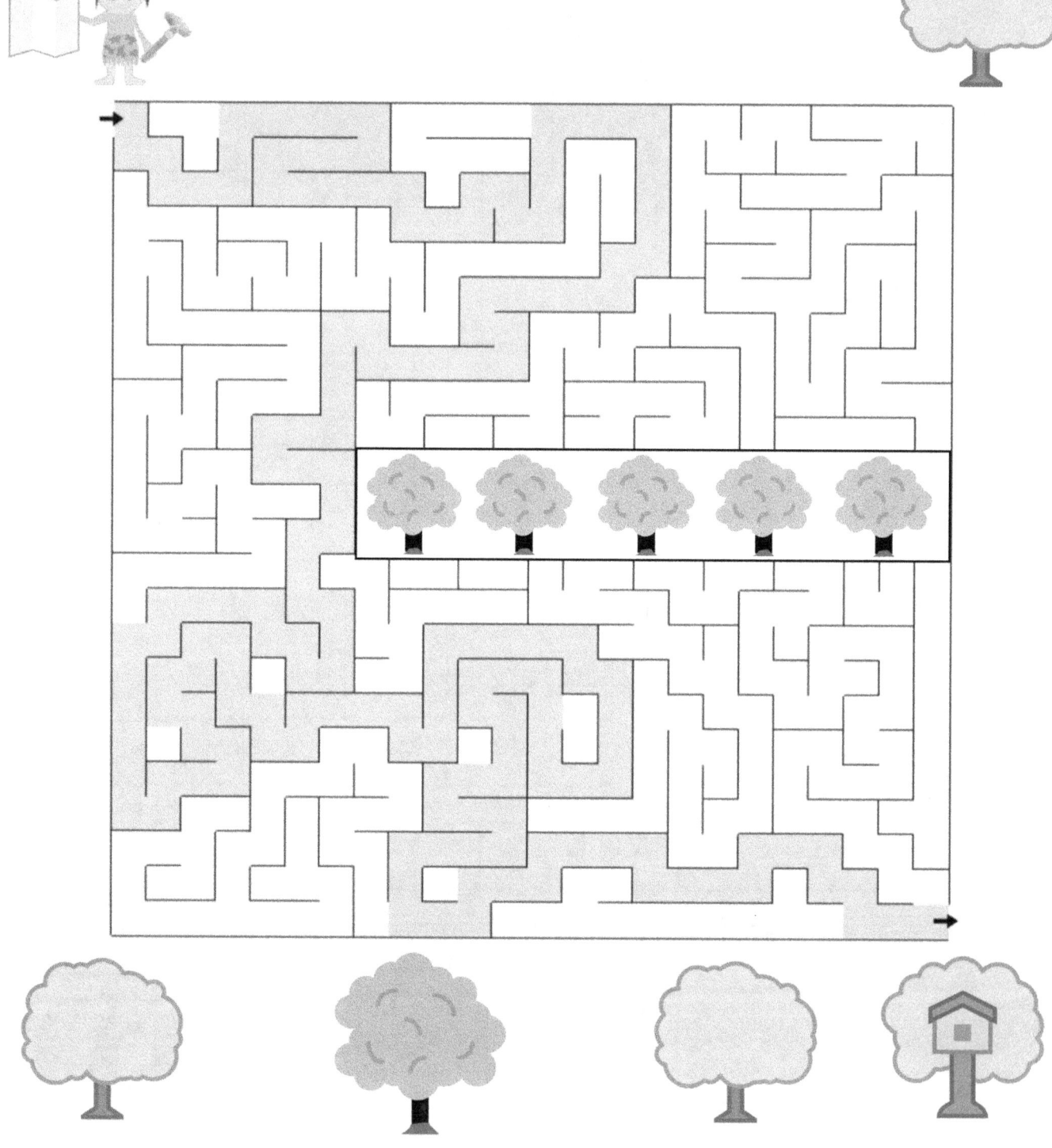

Kror's brother Aruk is in danger, rush to his rescue

Food sources are getting low. Dran heard of a new grain that grows well. Find it and plant it.

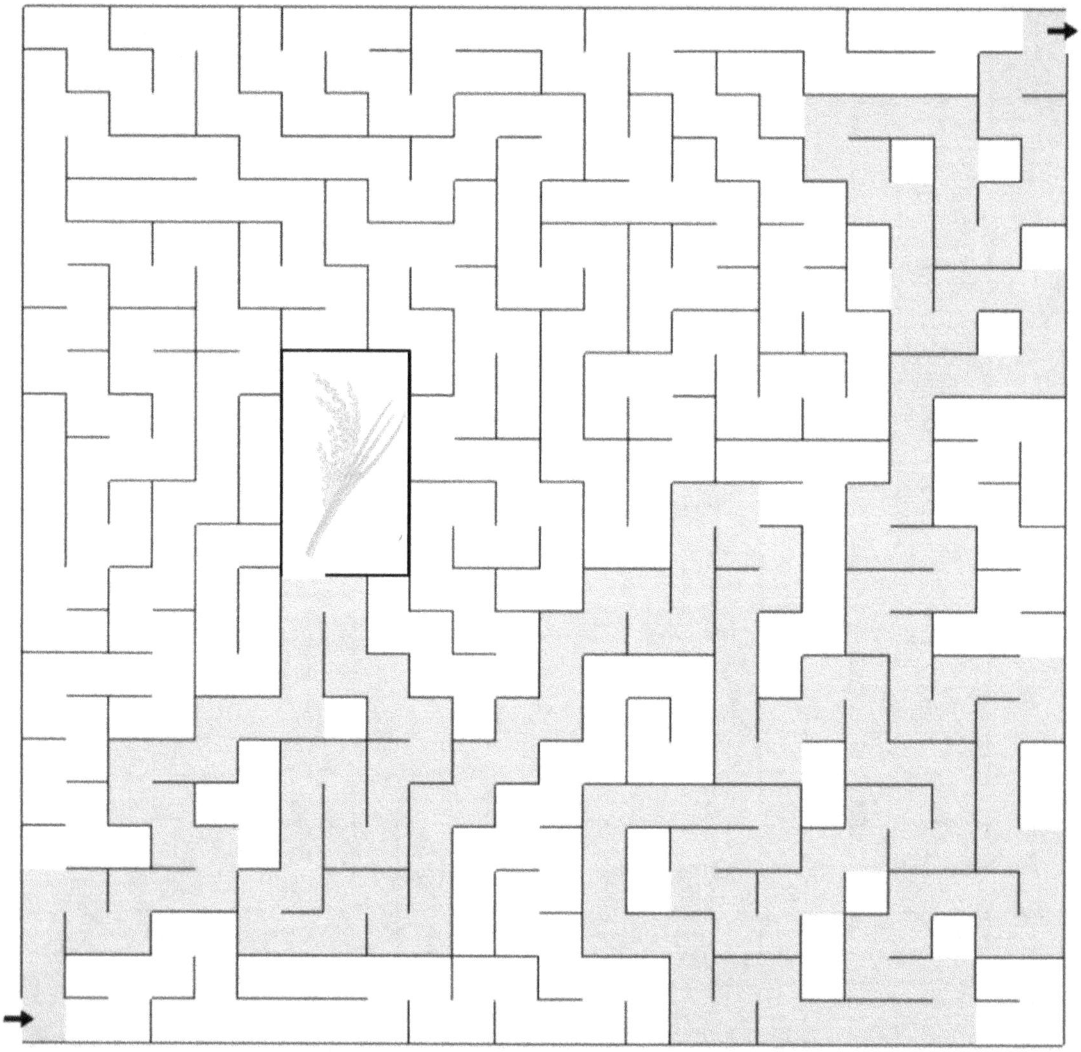

Kror tamed an animal for use in growing crops. Help Kror take the animal back to camp

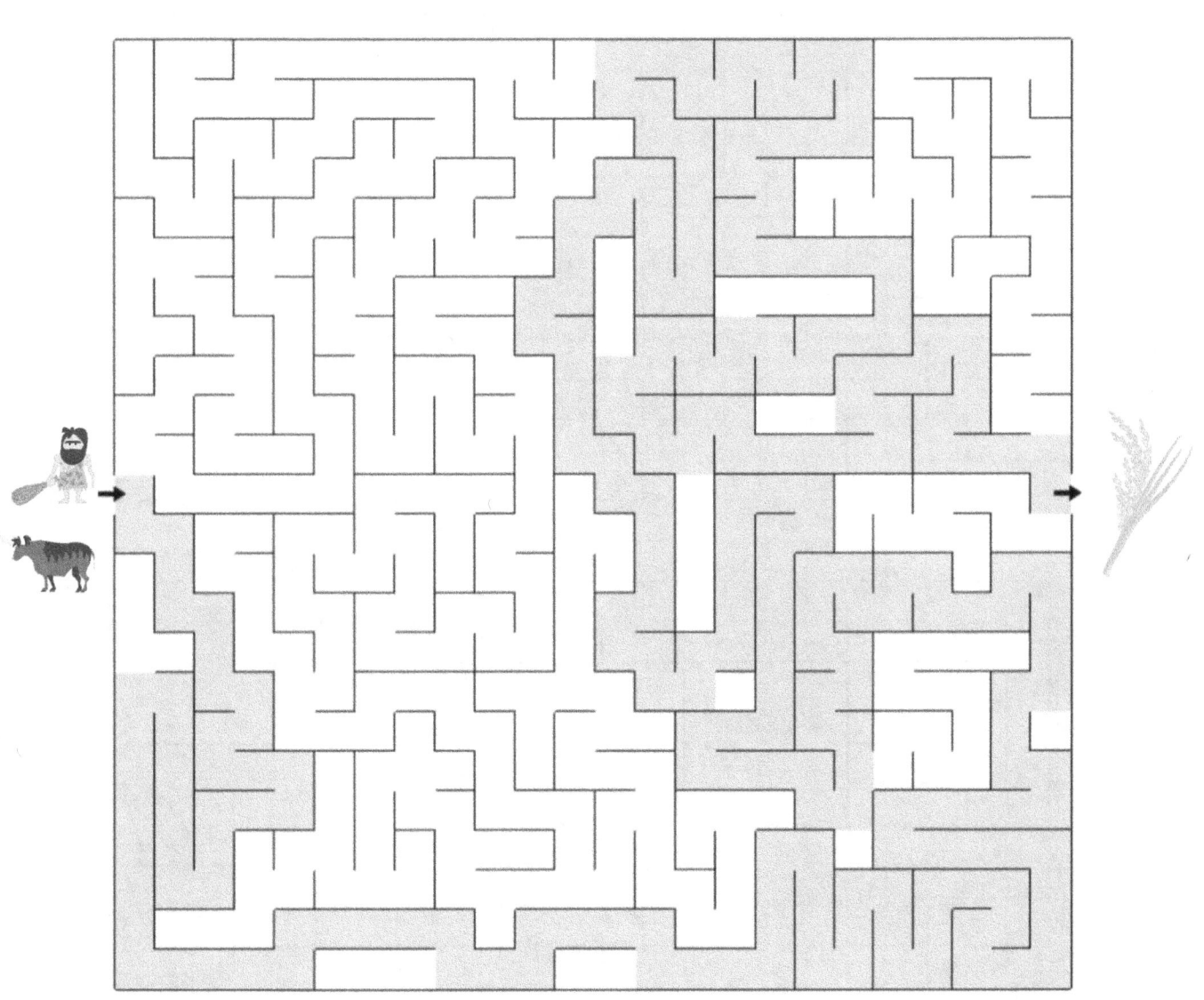

Terrible rains are coming and their animal has run off! Find the animal and get the Grobbles to safety in a nearby cave

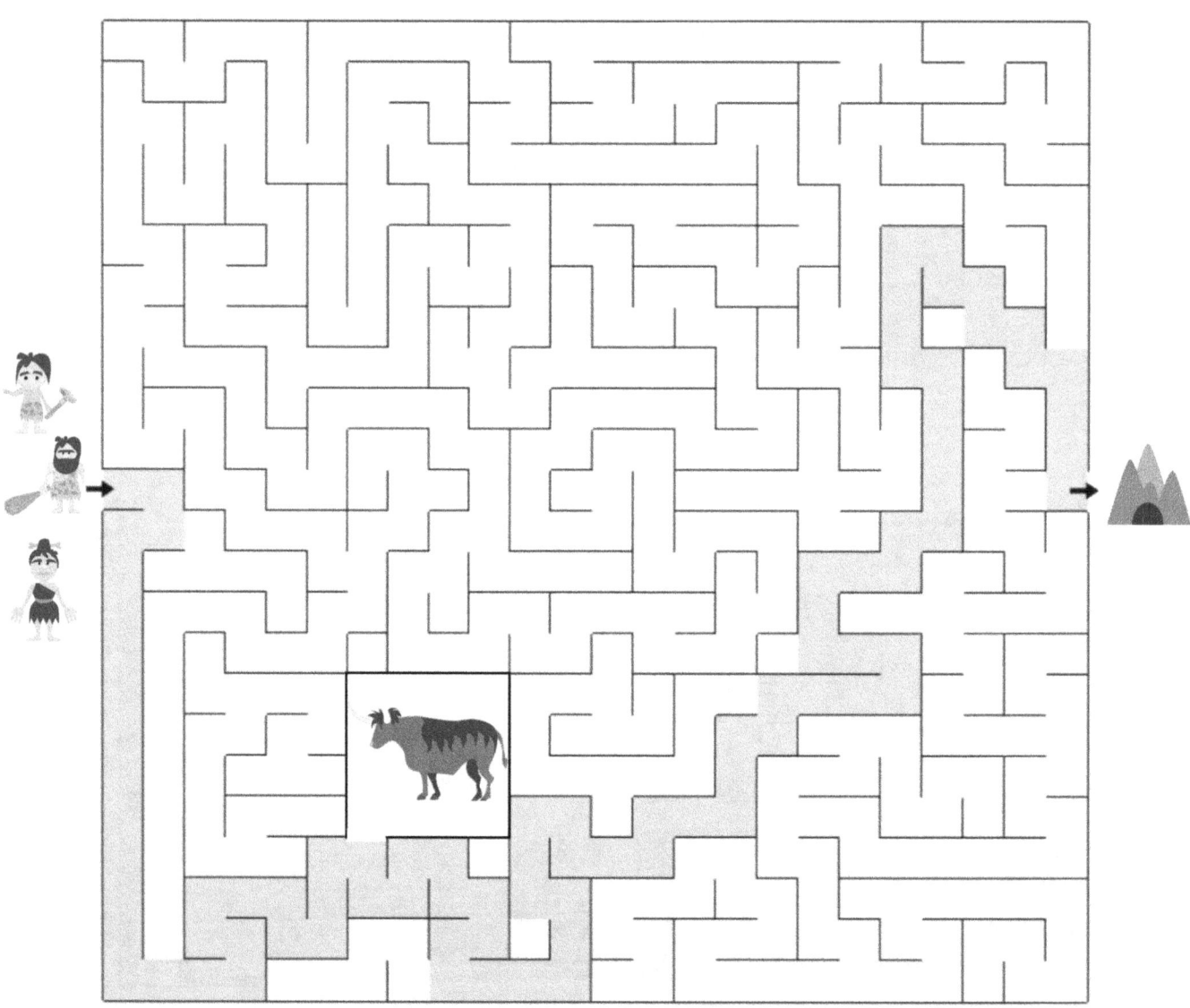

The land is filling with water too quickly! Cross the river and find new land

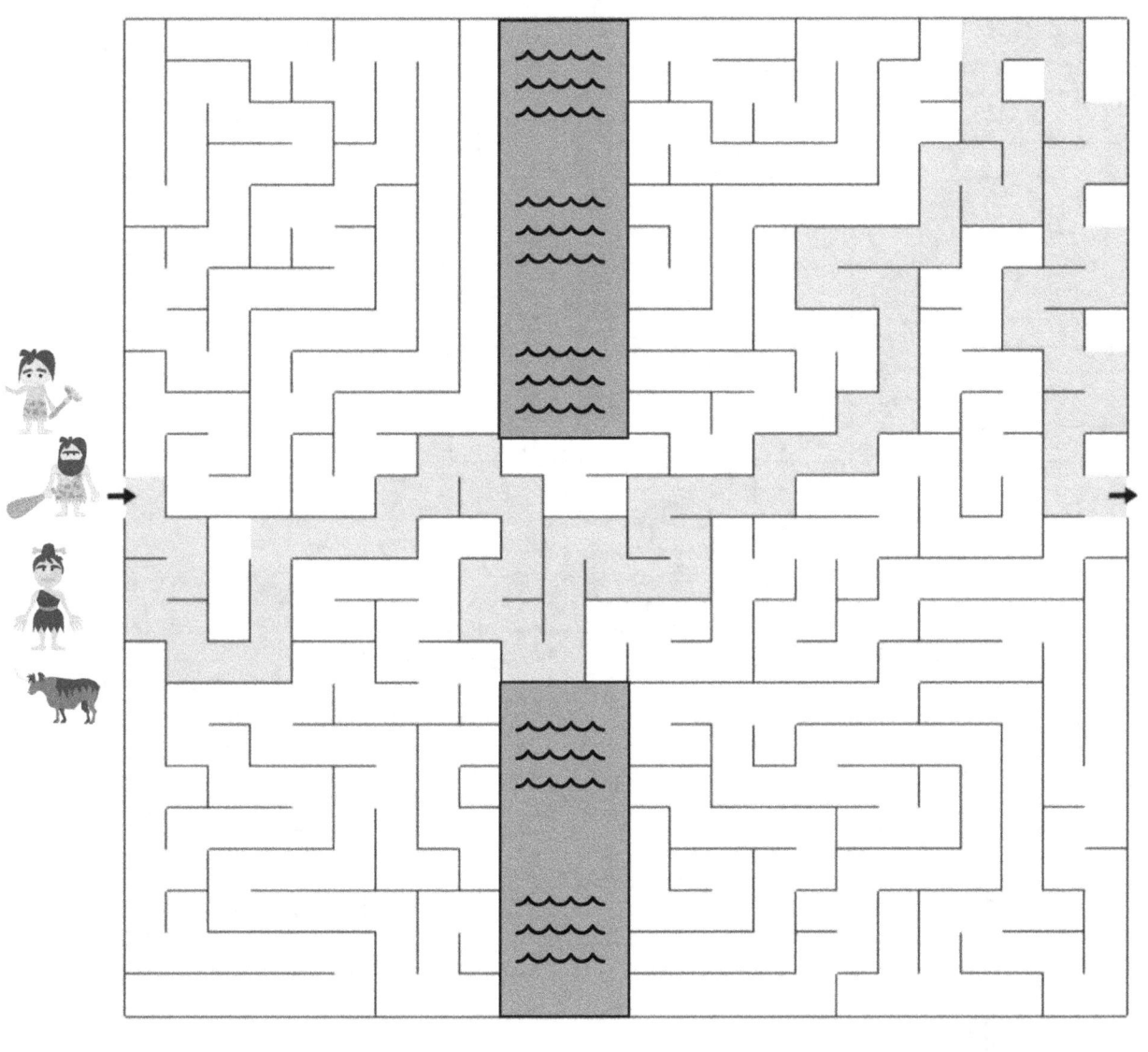

The wetlands are difficult to navigate. Avoid the crocodiles and find the big tree for shelter

Dran spotted a tree with new fruit on the way to the big tree ! Go back and fetch some fruit

Careful of the larger creatures here

Crik has fallen into a pond in the new wetlands, help him swim to safety

Aruk tried to follow the Grobbles family to the new big tree but got lost along the way. Help him find his way

Crik is scared of the new larger creatures. Go scare them off

With all of their crops washed away, Crik wants to release their tamed animal. Find a safe place to do so

Kror wants to surprise Dran with a rare flower. Go deeper in the forest and find it

Kror needs to find some vine to help put a new shelter together. Navigate through the palm trees to find some

Legend says a 'Great Axe' is hidden inside a cave. Help Kror find the cave

Careful of the big cats

You found the cave. The Great Axe is near but avoid the biting bats!

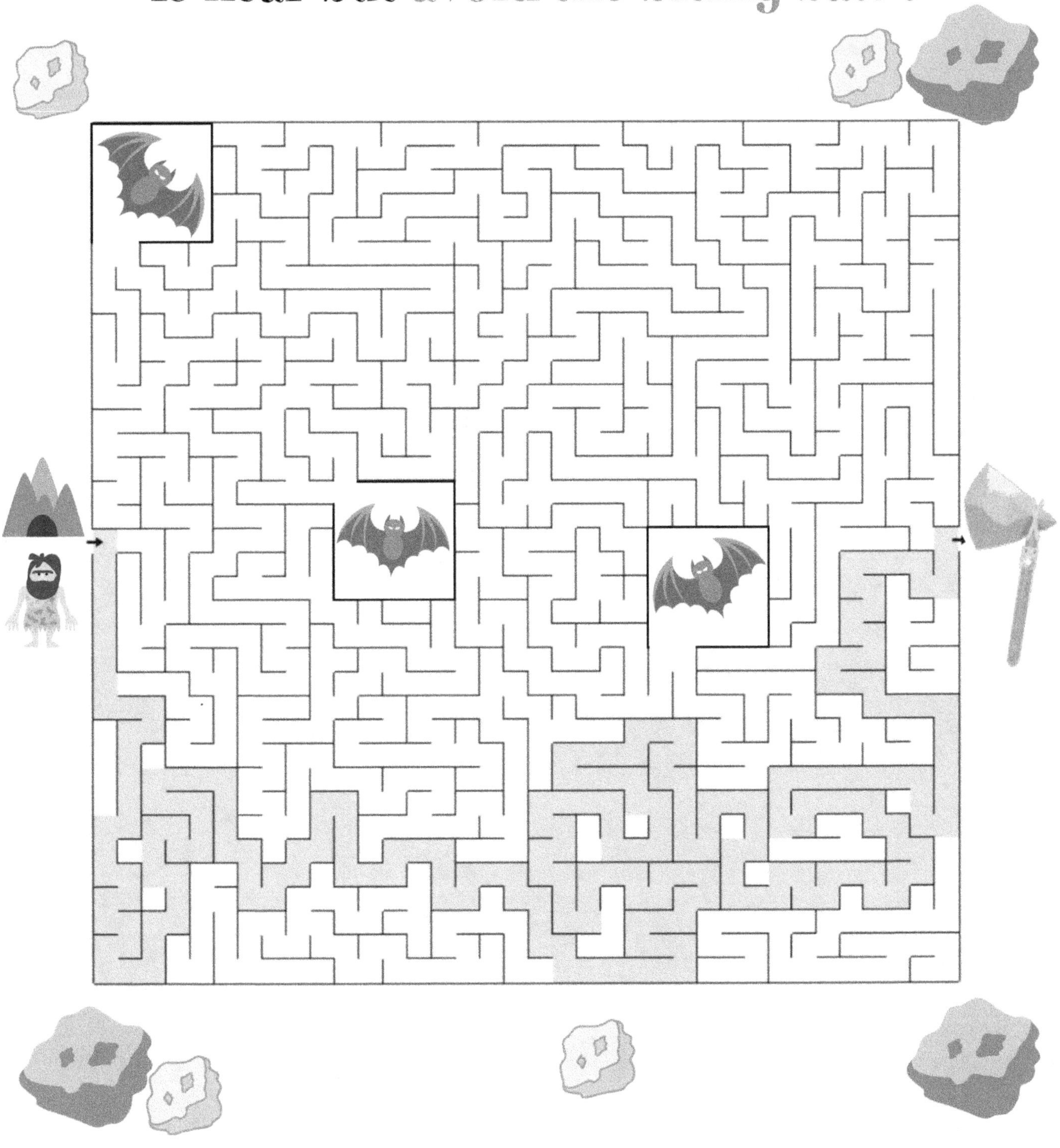

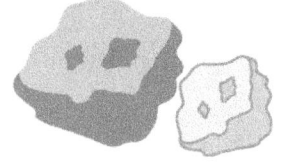

www.ingramcontent.com/pod-product-compliance
Lightning Source LLC
Chambersburg PA
CBHW081236080526
44587CB00022B/3960